Medicine, the Community, and Health

Robert F. Gloor
M.D.,M.PH., Editor

Cover design by
Louis Fuiano

To Kurt W. Deuschle, whose leadership in the areas of medicine, the community and health has been an inspiration to many and to whom we in the discipline of community medicine owe so much.

Contributors*

Terence R. Collins, M.D., M.P.H.; Professor, Department of Community Health and Family Medicine, University of Florida College of Medicine, Gainesville, FL, Health Programs Supervisor, District 3, Health and Rehabilitation Services, State of Florida

Roland P. Ficken, Ph.D.; Associate Professor and Chairman, Department of Behavioral Science

Robert F. Gloor, M.D., M.P.H.; Associate Professor, Department of Community Medicine

L. Ralph Jones, M.D.; Associate Professor and Chairman, Department of Psychiatry

Charles Konigsberg, Jr.; M.D., M.P.H., Director and Health Officer, Memphis and Shelby County Health Department, Memphis, TN

James D. Leeper, Ph.D.; Assistant Professor, Department of Community Medicine

Richard R. Parlour, M.D.; Associate Professor, Department of Psychiatry

Elizabeth R. Ruben, M.D.; Clinical Assistant Professor, Department of Community Medicine

F. Douglas Scutchfield, M.D.; Director and Professor of Public Health, School of Public Health, San Diego State University, San Diego, CA

Hunter G. Taft, M.S.S.E.; former Director of Environmental Health, West Alabama District Health Department, Tuscaloosa, AL, and Adjunct Instructor, Department of Community Medicine

---

*Unless otherwise stated, from the College of Community Health Sciences, University of Alabama, University, AL, 35486

Table of Contents

Why Community Medicine?

Robert F. Gloor, M.D., M.P.H.

Years ago, medical teaching was conducted very much in the community. However, the Flexner Report of 1910, resulted in the development of medical centers established in conjunction with universities and consolidated medical education in the university setting.[1] This movement strengthened the scientific education of the medical student and gave impetus to the association of research efforts with medical education but, at the same time, moved away from the community to the medical center, not only medical education but that of other health professionals. In the past 15 years various groups have called for the greater involvement of communities and community health professionals in the educational process of the health worker. The National Commission on Community Health Services pointed out the need for a personal physician who would integrate the care received by a patient, utilizing the various resources in the community as needed.[2] Such a physician would be aware of various social, emotional, and environmental factors influencing the health of the patient's family. Two other reports concerned with the education of physicians also stressed the need for utilization of the community and its resources in this education.[3,4]

While these reports focus on physicians, the implications are for all health professionals. This was recognized by the Carnegie Commission on the Future of Higher Education in 1970 when it recommended the development of area health education centers where health care personnel would be educated in a community setting that was tied to the university health science center.[5] All of these reports recognize the importance of the exposure of students of health careers to the needs of communities and the resources available or needed in order to solve community problems.

Along with the development of this emphasis on the utilization of community resources in the educational process of health personnel has been the development of a new, related but different, discipline in medicine—the field of community medicine. First formally established at the University of Kentucky in 1960, the concept of community medicine has progressed into reality.

Community medicine may be defined as "...that field of medicine concerned with improving the health of a total community through the identification and solution of its health problem."*

This was the definition when that first department of community medicine in a medical school was established. The focus was on the community instead of the individual patient or even on the family, the latter being the prerogative of family medicine.

As the field of community medicine was further developed, a multi-disciplinary approach was used and the definition broadened, although the emphasis remained on the community and the solution of its health problems. In 1968 community medicine was seen as:

> a cooperative integrated program of medical and biological disciplines for studying and solving in-depth community health problems. This includes an organized community effort in environmental health related specifically to fundamental causes and social consequences of all of the more prevalent diseases. In the final analysis the diagnosis and treatment of community and social pathology, not individual pathology, must be our major concern.§

In 1969, the core concept remained unchanged as community medicine was described as:

> the academic discipline that deals with the identification and solution of the health problems of communities or human population groups. This discipline, like internal medicine or pediatrics, has for its goal the solution of people's health problems through clinical application of the basic science disciplines of pathology, microbiology, behavioral sciences and biostatistics. However, community medicine considers people in groups or communities as well as individually, encompassing the traditional and relevant skills and knowledge of public health and preventive medicine along with the growing concern for the delivery of medical care. The epidemiologic method and body of knowledge are in a special position, linking the basic science portion of the discipline with the applied phase in the community.†

Each of these quotations adds to our understanding of community medicine. It is a discipline in medicine, focusing on the community for the purpose of identifying and solving its problems related to health, and utilizing the expertise of health professionals in a variety of fields in the solution of these problems. So while the term "community medicine" is used in this text, this use is not meant to minimize the important contributions many different health professionals make in this field. For purposes of this text, "community medicine" will refer to the discipline described above in its concern for

---

*From Deuschle KW: The concept of community medicine and heart disease. Bull NY Acad Med (49:451, 1973). Used by permission of the publisher and author.

§From Deuschle KW, Eberson F: Community medicine comes of age. J Med Educ (43:1229, 1968.) Used by permission of the publisher and author.

†From Tapp JW, Deuschle KW: The community medicine clerkship. Milbank Mem Fund Q 47:412, 1969. Used by permission of the publisher.

community health, which term broadly includes all aspects of the community which have a bearing on the wellbeing of the people of the community. In this respect, health is contrasted with sickness, and the concern of community medicine encompasses and extends beyond medical care services to include all activities contributing to optimal functioning of the citizenry. Priorities may indicate that certain more peripheral concerns receive less emphasis than those more directly related to sickness or health. Such decisions should be made, most properly, by the people of the community as they analyze their needs and concerns, and look at alternative solutions, assisted by the community medicine consultant.

Community medicine differs from medicine in the community in that its concern is with the group or community. A community is a gathering of people in a localized area, who are divided into various interacting groups and who share a consciousness of spatial unity and cultural semblance. The term community, is further discussed at length in Chapter 2. Community medicine accepts a broad definition of the word "health."

Community medicine, with its focus on the community, encompasses aspects of preventive medicine. Indeed, physicians who specialize in community medicine do so in one of the fields certified by the American Board of Preventive Medicine such as general preventive medicine or public health. The Board defines preventive medicine as a special field of medical practice which:

> 1) has a primary focus on health and disease as these occur in communities and in defined population groups;
> 2) seeks to promote those practices with respect to the community and the individual who will advance health, prevent disease, make possible early diagnosis and treatment, and foster rehabilitation of those with disabilities;
> 3) requires knowledge of the basic disciplines of biostatistics, epidemiology, administration and the social and environmental sciences in addition to the basic knowledge and skills required of a physician.*

Preventive medicine focuses more usually on the individual patient and his or her status but of course, at times utilizes the broader community approach. Public health programs have not been given the resources nor the mandate to fulfill the broad role encompassed in the concept of community medicine. Many public health officials recognize that ideally they should have a wider concern in all aspects pertaining to the community's health and are attempting to practice community medicine.

Community medicine differs from family practice because of its wider focus on group problems rather than on patients in a physician's office. However, particularly in a rural community, the physician in private practice and other health workers are confronted daily with opportunities to incorporate

---

Fifteenth Edition of the Bulletin of the American Board of Preventive Medicine, *December, 1976. Used by permission.*

community medicine into their practices. More formally this may be through membership on a health systems agency or public health board. The physician will become involved in professional standards review activity. However, as a leading citizen of the community, health workers will be looked to for leadership in many informal avenues related to health. With one hand on the pulse of the community (the patients in the office), the health professional should ever be alert for a wider significance of the illness or disability causing the patient to seek medical care. Community medicine, because of its broad viewpoint, has application to all disciplines of medicine as well as to those of other health professionals. Designed as an introduction to the field, this text should well serve the needs of the student of a health career who wishes for a broader viewpoint beyond individual patients and their problems.

In Chapter 2, Ficken discusses the ecological approach in community medicine and the development of a neighborhood clinic. He also tells of an epidemic in which the understanding of the community became vital to the control of the disease.

In Chapter 3, the differing patterns of disease, disability, and the utilization of health services by minority groups are introduced. The effect of reducing the financial barrier to care through the development of Medicare and Medicaid should be noted. This again emphasizes the importance of looking at many factors, not just one—in this case the financial.

Chapters 4 and 5 deal with two of the key disciplines utilized in community medicine. Collins' chapter will introduce the student to the principles of epidemiologic investigation and because of the importance as well as the depth of the field more space has been allocated to the topic. Leeper's chapter on biostatistics should serve as an introduction to this field, an understanding of which is so necessary in the proper investigation of a community's health problems or in applying the findings or patient oriented research data to large groups.

Chapter 6, on institutions and levels of care focuses on aspects of the current system of "health" care which is primarily "medical" care oriented. This is done in order to give the student an understanding of the present system at a time when there are many pressures on the system for change. The various types of organization for the delivery of ambulatory care services (health, maintenance organization, group practice, fee for service, prepaid service, etc.) are not discussed in this text, and for an understanding of these patterns of practice the student is referred to other sources.

In Chapter 7, Ruben discusses various categories of health manpower with a brief discussion of the concept of "team". With this background the student should be better prepared to understand current conflicts in the area of manpower for health services.

While Scutchfield does not discuss national health insurance, the material presented in Chapter 8 provides a background for a better understanding of the issues in the various proposals currently being discussed. As the title of the chapter states, the focus is on medical care costs. A broadening view of health and health care will undoubtedly require greater initial investment although in the long run savings should be achieved.

In Chapter 9, the increasing requirement for public accountability on the part of those providing health services is presented with more detailed discussion of the main current mechanisms for such accountability—the Health Systems Agency and the Professional Standards Review Organization. Principles of good health which are generally accepted are also given.

Konigsberg and Taft discuss, in Chapter 10, the role of the public health department in the provision of health care services including the monitoring of environmental concerns. The student should note the various limitations faced by the health department as it attempts to meet its responsibility to the community.

In Chapter 11, Collins provides much useful material for persons who become involved in occupational health services.

Jones and Parlour in Chapter 12, give a well referenced introduction to the current movement of mental health care from the institution to the community. There is also a lengthy discussion of prevention, the general principles of which apply to all fields of health services.

Other topics related to community medicine would be included were it not desirable to keep the text to a manageable size and one of service to the student being introduced to the field. The topics covered should create an awareness of the variety of concerns which are appropriate for the health professional's interest in the needs of the community which he or she serves.

REFERENCES

1. Flexner A: Medical Education in the United States and Canada: A Report to the Carnegie Foundation for the Advancement of Teaching. Boston, MA, The Merrymount Press, 1910.
2. Health is a community affair: Report of the National Commission on Community Health Services. Cambridge, MA, Harvard University Press, 1967.
3. The graduate education of the physician: The Report of the Citizens Commission on Graduate Medical Education. Chicago, IL, AMA, 1966.
4. Meeting the challenge of family practice: The Report of the *Ad Hoc* Committee on Education for Family Practice of the Council on Medical Education. Chicago, IL, AMA, 1966.
5. Higher education and the nation's health: Policies for medical and dental education: A Report of the Carnegie Commission on the Future of Higher Education. New York, NY, McGraw-Hill, 1970.

2

The Community in Community Medicine

Roland P. Ficken, Ph.D.

Community medicine is a rapidly growing and relatively young discipline within the framework of medical education. It involves a more global approach to the problems of health care than the traditional, single physician-patient model. Community medicine asks that individual problems be understood within the context of the community. In this sense, the community rather than the individual becomes the central unit of analysis, and thus the essential factor in a fuller understanding of the etiology of disease, the process of disease, those factors relevant to its prevention and treatment, and indeed, the nature of health.

Understanding health in the context of "community" is a broad, ambitious, and complex undertaking. Nevertheless, health and illness occur not only in the individual and in small groups, but in communities. Many of the variables which we know to be important to health and illness are unique to the social structure which we define as community. Thus, the community is a vital component of our knowledge base.

Definition of Community

A primary rule of the scientific enterprise is the precise definition of concepts. It is interesting that while a great deal of debate has recently occurred in academic medicine, and much of it by community medicine faculties, about the definition and boundaries of primary care, little thought has been given to defining the central focus of the discipline, the community.[1]

Why might that be the case? We assume, all of us, that "community" is a word about which we have a common understanding. It is, however, a word that has many shades of meanings. For example, some use the term to refer to factories, trade unions, corporations, professional communities, military communities, religious communities, academic communities, and so on. In fact, "community" is sometimes used to describe a moral or a spiritual phenomenon. All of these definitions are useful and acceptable depending upon their context. However, for our purposes and to avoid inconsistency and ambiguity, we need a definition which fits consistently with the functions and activities of community medicine. In this discussion, we will use "community" to refer to those units of social and territorial organization which, depending upon their size, can also be called hamlets, villages, towns, cities, counties, or metropolitan areas. In this definition, community refers to the places where people maintain their homes, earn their livings, rear their children, and carry out most of their life activities.[2] According to Hillery,[3] at least three major elements enter into most definitions of community including, 1) geographic area; 2) social interaction; and 3) common tie or ties. This definition gives us not only some sense of the internal components of a community, but also helps to establish a set of boundaries which distinguish one community from another.

The Ecological Approach in Community Medicine

Now that we have defined the primary unit of analysis, our next step should be an outline of the approach to the study of the community. Unlike many other disciplines within medicine, community medicine has elected a holistic approach to the study of health and illness, thus using broader units of analysis and wider frames of reference rather than increasingly narrower micro-explanations. That being the case, ecological theory is a most useful explanatory approach. Human ecology has been called the astronomy of human constellations.[4] As Bruhn has indicated, some have preferred to conceptualize human ecology as the sum total of numerous ecosystems which interlock and share reciprocal cause-effect pathways. The term ecosystem can be applied to a single cell, tissues, organs, organisms, or populations at levels of increasing organizational complexity; each can be considered an ecosystem if the total environment is added as an integral part of the system. A principle attribute of the human ecology approach is that one can only understand a given ecosystem by viewing it in the context of the larger composite of ecosystems. What all of this really means is that everything affects everything else. In this framework, the data base would seem to be almost infinite. Such a methodology for studying the problems of community medicine appears staggering; however, the first thing a student of man's condition must recognize is that complex problems have complex answers. There are no simple solutions to the problems of health and illness. However, there must be a way to order these expansive concepts into manageable categories for investigation.

For the purposes of community medicine, an ecological analysis of a community involves four broad variables: 1) sociocultural; 2) psychological; 3) physical; 4) biological. Under each of these primary variables, there are numerous subcategories. For example, *sociocultural* subsumes population, age and sex distribution, marital status, family structure, social stratification, economic, political, and religious structures, along with several others. *Psychological* includes behavior patterns and group behavior or social interaction. The *physical* involves location and geography, terrain, climate, water supply, and so forth. And finally, the *biological* includes such factors as nutrition, fertility rates, birth rates, histories of infectious diseases, and chronic illnesses.[4] A complete analysis of a community utilizing these subsystems and the results of their interactions characterize the ecological approach to the community. Whether one is interested in the total health of the community or in the etiology and effect of a single disease within a community, this method of analysis provides the most complete understanding and thus delineates the greatest number of alternatives for intervention.

To give some pragmatic substance to this brief review of the community and human ecology, it is useful to examine the methodology within the context of some case studies. The first example will deal with a specific disease problem within a community; the second, from Dubos,[5] with global ramifications of interdependent systems.

In the summer of 1975, there were spotty outbreaks of Saint Louis Encephalitis in Mississippi in several towns close to the Mississippi River. The following year, the summer of 1976, a number of cases occurred in Alabama, and in time, the Southport area.* Eventually, there was concern over the possibility of the disease reaching epidemic proportions. Although the vectors and chain of infection are fairly well known (virus reservoir in bird populations → mosquitoes → human infection), from the ecological perspective, the interesting aspect of the outbreak of Saint Louis Encephalitis in Southport was the number of ecosystems it involved.

Almost all of the cases occurred among persons of lower socioeconomic status on the city's west side, a predominately black population. In this area of the city, drainage has been a problem for years. Following heavy rains, water stands in ditches for weeks at a time and becomes an ideal breeding ground for mosquitoes. In addition, the neighborhoods are profusely cluttered with cans, bottles, and old tires, all reservoirs for water which become infested with mosquito larvae. The people, by virtue of longstanding cultural patterns, spend a great deal of time visiting with neighbors out-of-doors into the late hours of the evening. Many homes are without screens, and very few have air conditioning, so windows are left open during the hot summer months, and mosquitoes become the constant companions of the inhabitants. Obviously, the prime population at risk, should a reservoir of the virus occur in the area, would be a population with these characteristics.

What is important for our understanding is the interrelationships of the

The community name has been changed to assure the anonymity of individuals and institutions.

systems. First of all, this economically deprived population lacks the resources to screen windows and doors, much less provide air conditioning systems which would allow for closed doors and windows and reduce the chance of infection from mosquitoes. Second, political power necessary to move city government to construct proper drainage systems is lacking as is often the case among minority groups in our society. Third, cultural factors which encourage walking from neighbor to neighbor and visiting on the front porch into the late hours of the evening (the prime time for infection from mosquitoes) are longstanding and very likely useful components for entertainment and communication, both factors which help to cement the community together.

All of these dimensions operate in such a way as to put the community at risk to particular kinds of disease problems. However, the same factors which put the community at risk provide the additional new sites for intervention. And this we have learned from studying the community instead of the virus.

Another example of the interrelation of systems comes to us from Rene' Dubos' account of the potato blight which broke out in Europe, and particularly in Ireland, around 1845.[5] The blight occurred because of the combination of a symbiotic, parasitic mold infestation of the potato and unusual weather conditions which changed the relationship of the mold to the potato in such a way that it became pathogenic. Two years of the blight and consequently a much reduced production of the potato was sufficient to ruin the economy of Ireland. Based primarily on the new food source of the potato, the Irish population had risen from about 3.5 million in 1700 to 8 million in 1840. Because of the blight and the acute food shortage, millions of persons died of outright starvation, and many others became more susceptible to a variety of infectious diseases because of poor nutrition. For that reason, a great epidemic of tuberculosis occurred throughout the Emerald Isle. The lack of food and the attendant economic misery also forced great numbers of Irish to immigrate, particularly to America, and it is this immigration that is primarily responsible for "transforming Pat, the Irish pig-tender, into a New York City cop." Rene' Dubos concludes his discussion of the weather, the potato blight, and the destiny of the Irish with this note:

> If ever a writer succeeds in making a popular story of the potato blight, he may conclude, as Tolstoy did for Napoleon's invasion of Russia, that its determinism is beyond human analytical power. In fact, it is perhaps just an illusion of science to believe that the vagaries of the relations between the potato and a microscopic fungus, inadequate farming practices, and the weather condition in the 1840s were the real factors that led the adventurous spirit of man to establish on the American continent the wit of the Irish, their Catholic faith, and their potential genius.*

---

*From Dubos: Mirage of Health, 1959. Courtesy of Harper & Row, publishers.

Community in Community Medicine

This is a classic example of the interdependence of systems. It should serve as a reminder to us that any tinkering we do with one system affects another, and the results may either be grand or disasterous—or a bit of both. The next section gives us an example of both kinds of results. It also deals with the interrelationships of socio-political systems and their influence upon behavior. The development of a primary health care center in an economically deprived area provides us with a case study example of the ecological process at another level of human experience—building community institutions.

History of a Community Health Center

A socioeconomical study of most communities will reveal demographic/ environmental niches which are medically indigent. Southport is not an exception. The people living in this community's west end are primarily black, low income, many well below poverty level, and usually without primary medical care other than what can be found in the Community Hospital Emergency Room. Many from this section of the city suffer chronic illnesses, such as congestive heart failure and hypertension, receive acute care in the Emergency Room, are released back into the community without scheduled follow-up, and eventually return to the hospital when their disease again becomes critical. This cyclical process occurs essentially because the population lacks accessibility to and availability of primary health care within their local environment. Medical students from the university recognized the health care problems of west end citizens through their contact with them in the Emergency Room and began to search with their faculty for ways to intervene. A decision was made to involve the community from the beginning.

One of the first steps the students and faculty undertook was to identify community representatives who had a broad interest in community affairs. Several persons with a background of leadership were found, all of whom expressed concern about health problems in the community. They asked to meet and discuss various strategies for improving the availability of care.

There were two objectives associated with the development of a "Community Committee". The first was to assess their support for a student-staffed "free clinic". Such a service would be operated one night per week with on-site coverage by a licensed M.D. from the college faculty or the private sector. The community representatives were overwhelmingly enthusiastic. The second objective was to determine the feasibility of using a student-staffed clinic and the "Community Committee" as a focal point around which something more substantial could be established to provide medical and social services to the indigent in Southport.

The development of the student project was a relatively new task. A building was secured through a community service agency, and the student clinic initiated service based on funding from community donations and the loan of equipment and some supplies from the college. Shortly after the clinic opened, the possibility for federal funding arose. The "Community Committee" was incorporated as a nonprofit organization and became the Board of Directors of the Southport Community Health Center. Several Board members were added for a total of nineteen. All officers of the Board— Chairman, Vice-Chairman, Secretary, and Treasurer—were black. All of the health professionals on the Board were white, and that group included two physicians. The black members of the Board included retired educators, an attorney, a mental health worker, a painter and clergymen.

Faculty and administrators with the college prepared a proposal to DHEW asking for funding to develop a primary health care center on Southport's west side, aimed principally at a target population defined by three census tracts. A budget of over $440,000 for three years was outlined with nearly half that amount requested for the first year. The Center would rely on clinic income and the development of other funding sources after the third year. The Board was not involved in any way with the proposal preparation and approved the final document with only an opportunity to scan its contents (40 pages) at a Board meeting.

The proposal was funded with only one week between notification and project initiation. Since no action could be taken until official notice was received, there was nearly two months' delay in the appointment of a full-time project director. As soon as official HEW notification arrived, a racially balanced Search Committee was appointed, with two black and two white members. Out of 15 applicants for the position, only one was a black, a woman, and this candidate became the project's first director. Prior to her arrival, a building had been secured, a rental agreement entered into, and initial renovation plans devised. DHEW officials previewed the drawings and suggested that an architect finalize the plans for formal approval. The project director, of course, assumed this task along with all other administrative matters associated with the development of the facilities and the clinic.

The project moved along rather well during its pre-funded days and during the first two months under the HEW grant. There appeared to be notable progress week by week. In fact, a survey of newspaper reports during the initiation of the Community Committee, the grant development, and final funding support the notion that all was going well with this "community-based" effort. In addition to the usual newspaper articles, the project even garnered the support of an editorial on two occasions. However, from the second until the eigth month of the federal support, almost all development appeared to cease. It became evident with each Board meeting that the project was falling further behind schedule. Architectural plans had not been presented to the Board, physician recruitment was stymied, and a number of administrative decisions made by the project director appeared to be inadequate in the judgement of the Board.

There was a concern that access to the Board was somewhat awkward for the project director. In an effort to enhance communication, an Executive Committee was named and asked to facilitate Board decisions needed by the project director. However, matters still did not seem to progress satisfactorily, and by the end of the eighth month, following a four hour meeting with the project director, the Executive Committee recommended to the Board that she be asked to resign. The Board agreed.

The project director would not resign and was subsequently removed from the position by Board action. It was not until this point that a clear division among black members of the Board became evident. Three black Board members resigned.

In the two months following the project director's dismissal, a physician member of the Board served as acting director and during this period of time, finalization of the architect's drawings, their approval by DHEW, the advertising and letting of bids for renovation, and the initiation of renovation all took place. The renovation moved very quickly, and was nearly complete by the beginning of the eleventh month.

In the meantime, a new Search Committee for Project Director was organized. This committee was composed of one white and four black Board members. By the eleventh month, a new project director had been named, a black woman. Fourteen months from initiation of funding the Center, temporarily staffed by residents from a family practice program, was receiving patients and most of the problems appeared to be resolved.

This brief history of the early development of a community health center points out a number of problems. The following analysis deals with those difficulties that occurred after federal funding was initiated.

Analysis

Attempts to enlist community participation in health services is by no means new in the American health care system. In fact, there are reports of this kind of involvement which go as far back as the American Revolution.[6] This is a pattern that does not appear to have reached its zenith; as a matter of fact, there will more than likely be an increasing demand for lay participation in many areas of society, presently exclusively controlled by various professions and/or the government. We will not attempt to argue the rationale for such participation, but rather simply review this case to determine if factors working against successful community involvement can be identified.

Paap believes that structural components play a significant role in the effectiveness of consumer-based boards in health centers.[7] He has suggested at least five major structural problems. The institutional structuring of *information, time,* the structural basis of *contacts* and *careers,* the lack of *political power bases,* and *organizational requisites* all appear to cause particular difficulty for community representatives.

There is little doubt that these factors played a role in lessening the full integration of community members in the development of the Southport Community Health Center. For example, the institutional structuring of information was a factor in the development of the original grant proposal. The college participants in the grant development did not feel compelled to involve community Board members in its preparation because it was believed that the language and format would be entirely foreign to them. Time is an obvious factor in the development of a grant proposal. Other structural variables were also important in inhibiting cohesiveness and participation such as the social and political structure of the community and especially the contemporary social and political ecology. The role of these elements of the human ecology of Southport was significant to the development and eventual outcome of the community health care center. The issues are not entirely unique to this case and perhaps have value for generalization to similar efforts in other communities.

Very little was known about communication patterns and the social and political structure of the black community (or for that matter the white community) in Southport. No studies were available on housing patterns, communication patterns, the political process, or the attitudes and values of the Southport people regarding the major institutions of social life, which would of course include matters related to health. So, there was almost no useful information concerning the social and political nature of the black community at the critical time of project initiation. Board members were selected without any understanding of their interrelationships with respect to political power bases within the community. Indeed, college faculty involved in the development of the Board were completely naive with regard to the existence of the various political movements in the community.

A major avenue of communication within this black community resides within the religious structure. While where was some inkling that this was the case, and two black ministers were named to the Board in its early stages, it was not understood that there were significant rivalries and even strong differences between churches, and their clergy and members.

The project was also being developed at a time when the black community in Southport felt a strong need to become more vocal and demonstrative regarding their participation in the broader community's social and institutional concerns. Thus, the environment was right for blacks to speak out energetically in situations where they believed that a member of their community was not receiving due consideration, or the powerful white community was making a token effort, or for that matter viewed as taking a paternalistic approach to their special needs. The best evidence of this mood in the community was represented by the formation of a strong civil rights group attached to the National Association for the Advancement of Colored People and the Southern Christain Leadership Conference. In addition to the general mood of the community, the social environment during this particular period of time had been somewhat ususually interrupted. A general referendum was called in Southport to decide whether or not to change the city form of government from a commissioner to a council structure. Such a change would give significantly greater representation to minority groups not currently included in the governmental process. Interestingly enough, the black community apparently became involved in this process in such a way that they eventually defeated their own goals. Without any assurance that the council form would be successful in the general referendum, squabbles developed within the black community around individuals who wished to run for the yet to be realized council positions. So much furor and debate were generated around these personalities that it interfered with a concerted effort to bring the black vote to the polls for the referendum. A change to the council form of government was defeated during the general election, leaving the black community upset and thwarted in the attempt to gain a voice in their affairs.

Two other divisive problems occurred within the broader community during this time. The school system, which to this point was partially integrated, was ordered by a federal judge to complete the desegregation process. The black community became deeply involved in the solution to this particular issue. And, a city commission dictated change in the garbage collection system, also generating unrest because so many Sanitation Department employees were black.

All of these issues had a combined and significant effect on the socio-political ecology of the community, and consequently upon the Board of Directors of the Southport Community Health Center. Various factions within the community were represented on the Board, and divisions over the broader issues seemed to become associated with or confused with Center problems, especially one as delicate as the request for resignation of the project director. All this contributed to polarity among the Board members.

Could such problems have been avoided if a better understanding of the socio-political ecology of the community had been available? The answer should be a qualified "yes". If it had been understood initially that the black community was not a solidified group as white Board members naively believed, the opportunity for a more open form for discussion could have been presented. Indeed, the Center and its goals should have a solidifying rather than a divisive effect in the community. Instead, the actual issues involving the development of the Center never received an objective review, but became additional fuel to the fire for strife within the black community.

"Forewarned is forearmed." This is a simple enough precept. Nevertheless, it may be the most critical initial step to take in the development of a community-based health care center. So often the process is rushed because of the structural constraints mentioned by Paap with respect to funding time frames and the unfortunate "crisis orientation" of our health care delivery system. Adequate time must be devoted to thoroughly understanding the socio-political ecology of the target community.

Another area which the experience of this Board would suggest needs some attention has to do with involvement in the *work* of the Center. While community Board members can take pride in their role in the development of a primary health care facility for their constituency, a continued, active, and useful involvement in Board affairs must be generated by a vested interest greater than this somewhat distant political contribution. Community Board members should be educated as thoroughly as possible in the actual *work* of the Center, and then be encouraged to pursue an active role of responsibility for particular areas of that *work* as it relates to the Board. Such a vested interest would very likely reduce the diffuse dispute over the entire operation. Everyone would have, to use the Madison Avenue phrase, "a piece of the rock."

Finally, consumers on the Board were consumers more often in the sense that they met the legal requirements, ethnicity and geography of residence. They are socially important people in the community but not necessarily consumers. Persons actually being served by the Center should comprise a substantial portion of the consumer composition of the Board. They naturally have vested interest in its oganization and development. The consumers of a primary health care center for a medically indigent population most likely have fewer among their numbers with personal political agenda, if for no other reason than that they are so engaged in the day-to-day acquisition of the essentials of life, they have little time to invest in other areas. This is not to disparage a role in the political scene, but to point out a social reality.

To briefly summarize approaches to community-based boards in health center development, the following points should be considered:
1) Allowances should be made for variation in the *structural* matters of *information, time, careers,* and *organizational imperatives;* 2) Initiators should have at hand and utilize as much data as possible concerning *communication patterns* and the *social* and *political ecology* of the community; 3) Project initiators should be aware of concurrent *institutional changes* in the target community; 4) Board members should have a *work*

responsibility liasion to the health center; and 5) "Actual" consumers should comprise a substantial proportion of the consumer membership of the Board.

These factors will vary by place and time but will all be present to some degree. They have been derived within an ecological framework and hopefully are general enough to translate to similar situations.

The answer to man's health and illness and the most effective ways in which we might intervene are complex. Community medicine has before it the task of analyzing health problems at this complex level. Its outcome should be as promising as the results of the ultracentrifuge, and at the same time should be complementary to all other systems of investigation within the health sciences.

Glossary

Community — Units of social and territorial organization which, depending on their size, may also be called hamlets, villages, towns, cities, or metropolitan areas. Three major elements usually enter into a definition of community: 1) geographic area; 2) social interaction; and 3) common tie or ties.

Ecology — The mutual relations between organisms and their environment. The word was coined by Ernst Haeckel, a biologist in 1870.

Ecosystem — The complex of a community and its environment functioning as a unit in nature.

Holistic — Emphasizing the organic or functional relation between parts and wholes.

Human Ecology — The sum of numerous ecosystems which interlock and share reciprocal cause-effect pathways. A principle attribute of the human ecological approach is that one can only understand a given ecosystem by viewing it in the context of the larger composite of ecosystems.

REFERENCES

1. Baker WH (ed): Preventive and Community Medicine in Primary Care. US Government Printing Office, 1978.
2. Poplin DE: Communities. New York, NY, The Macmillian Company, 1972, p 3.
3. Hillery GA: Definitions of community: Areas of agreement. Rural Sociol 20:118, 1955.
4. Bruhn JC: Human ecology in medicine. Environ Res 3:37—53, 1970.
5. Dubos R: Mirage of Health. New York, NY, Harper & Row, Publishers, 1959, pp 86—90.
6. Notkin H, Notkin MS: Community participation in health services, a review article. Med Care Rev 27:1178, 1970.
7. Paap WR: Consumer-based boards of health centers: Structural problems in achieving effective control. A J Pub Health 68:578—582, 1978.

BIBLIOGRAPHY

Jonas S: Limitations of community control of health facilities and service. A J Pub Health 68:541-543, 2978.

Kane RL: The Challenges of Community Medicine. New York, NY, Springer Publishing Company, 1974.

Lee D: Environmental health and human ecology. A J Pub Health 54:7, 1964.

Lee D: An ecological approach to environmental health services. Bioscience 15:524, 1965.

Minorities and Health Care

3

Robert F. Gloor, M.D., M.P.H.

Background

All segments of our society do not experience the same health status, perceive the same needs, nor utilize health services to the same degree and in the same manner. The poor usually have received health care at a different level than others. This has been based partly on financial ability, but cultural factors have also played an important role. A number of minority groups existing today are different in these areas from the majority of Americans. These minorities include racial and ethnic groups, the elderly, low income, and rural populations. However, the main factors identifying each of these groups interact, and it is usually difficult to associate any one factor as the sole reason for an identified difference. This chapter will look at the interrelationships among certain demographic factors, perceived health status, morbidity and mortality statistics and the utilization of health services among selected minority groups.

Ethnic and racial minorities comprised 16.8% of the U.S. population in 1970.[1] These 34 *plus* million people include the blacks (11.1%), those with Spanish surnames or Hispanics (4.5%), Asian Americans (0.8%), Native Americans (0.4%) and other non-white Americans (0.1%). In 1975, 12.3% of all Americans were below the poverty level; however, 29.3% of persons in racial minorities were below the poverty level.[2]

Another minority group is the elderly, those 65 years of age or over, estimated to comprise 10.8% of the U.S. population in 1977. The black and Hispanic populations have smaller percentages of elderly (7.5% and 4.2% respectively), probably due to family size and more children.[3] This is also reflected in dependency ratios for the various groups. The ratios used here represent the population under age 18 and over age 64 divided by the population age 18 through age 64. With exception of Asian Americans, with a dependency ratio of 0.63, the racial and ethnic minorities all have higher dependency ratios than that of white Americans, at 0.77. For blacks, the ratio is 0.97, for Spanish origin Americans, 0.95 and for native Americans, 1.04.[1]

19

Health Status

The Health Interview Survey, conducted by the Public Health Service, provides information useful in comparing the perceived health status of individuals in the various population groups. In 1975 minorities (18.1%) were more likely to consider their health to be fair or poor than whites (11.6%), and blacks (19.0%) were even more likely to than the minorities as a whole.[4] This was also true for all respondents with low income; 27.4% of those with family income of less than $3,000 reported fair or poor. This percentage decreases gradually to 5.1% of those with an income over $25,000. Blacks and racial minorities also had more restricted activity days and more bed disability days than did whites (Table 3.1).

TABLE 3.1

Number of Restricted Activity Days and Bed Disability
Days Per Person Per Year by Race U.S., 1975*

	Restricted Activity Days	Bed Disability Days
Blacks	21.4	9.2
Racial Minority	20.4	8.8
Whites	17.5	6.2

*Adapted from: Health of the Disadvantaged, Department of Health, Education and Welfare, 1977, p 28.

The lowest income group had more than three times the number of restricted activity days and bed disability days than did the highest income group. As one might expect, 1974—76 estimates based on the Health Interview Survey show the same type of correlation with increasing age (Table 3.2). Work loss days are also experienced more frequently by the low income and racial minority groups.[2]

Mortality

The previous figures on disability are all based on samples, and the differences are considered to be significantly underestimated. They also represent self-assessment of the respondent's status, rather than objective determinations. However, there are real differences in a number of reported events, where figures may be more firm. Death rates are higher in non-whites than in whites, and this difference exists for both males and females (Figure 3.1). There has been a decline in the death rates with some leveling off of these rates in the mid-1950s. The rate for non-white males is one third greater than for white males. Non-white females experience an age adjusted rate 50% higher than white females.

Minorities and Health Care

TABLE 3.2

Estimates of Percent of Persons with Limited
Activity due to Chronic Conditions U.S., 1974-1976*

Age	Limited in Activity	Limited in† Amount or Kind of Major Activity	Unable to† Carry On Major Activity
Under 45 years	6.7	3.3	0.7
45-64	24.0	13.2	5.7
65 years and older	46.0	22.4	17.3

*Adapted from: State Estimates of Disability and Utilization of Medical Services:
U.S. 1974-1976, Department of Health, Education and Welfare, August 1978, p 4.

†Included in Column One.

From 1920 to 1976 the percent increase in life expectancy at birth in non-whites (50.8%) was one and one half times greater than that in whites (33.9%); however, in 1976 non-whites could expect to live 68.3 years compared to 73.5 years for whites. Non-white males had a life expectancy 8.0% less than white males while the difference in females was 5.3%.[2,4]

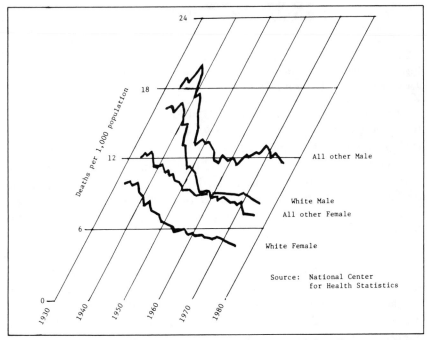

Fig. 3.1. Age-adjusted death rates, by color and sex, 1933—73. (From: Health in the United States, 1975. DHEW, 1976.)

Robert Gloor

21

Blacks experience an infant mortality rate 80% higher than whites (Figure 3.2). In 1974 maternal mortality was three and one half times higher in blacks than in whites. For both whites and minorities, infant mortality was higher in poverty areas compared to non-poverty areas of the same city, and both income and education of the father appear to play a greater role than race alone.[2]

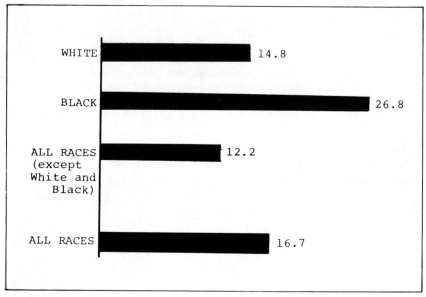

Fig. 3.2. Infant mortality rates by race, US 1974. (Adapted from: Health of the Disadvantaged. DHEW, 1977, p 67.)

There are differences in the causes of death according to race. Most rates for the leading causes of death are higher in non-whites than in whites. For example, in 1975, the death rate due to accidents was 32% higher in non-whites (that for deaths due to fires and conflagrations was 140% higher, in 1976—1977). However, the suicide death rate was 43.6% less in non-whites than in whites.[5] Death rates for violent causes are 90% higher in poverty areas than in non-poverty areas. The homicide rate for racial minorities is 742% that for whites.[2]

Morbidity

In 1974, case rates for newly reported tuberculosis in racial minorities were nearly five times those for whites.[2] For males the rates were 13.1 per 100,000 for whites and 61.2 for racial minorities; for females, 6.4 and 30.3 respectively. Certain other diseases are also more common among minorities. For example, hypertension is 66% more prevalent among blacks than whites.[6]

Minorities and Health Care

In some areas, minorities may show a better health status than do whites. For example, the findings concerning decayed, missing and filled teeth in a study conducted from 1960 to 1962,[2] show that blacks had more fillings per person, but fewer missing or carious teeth. Periodontal disease was more common among blacks of both sexes. In addition, even though in the nutrition survey of 1972 blacks showed a greater number of deficiencies of vitamins A, C, and D, iron, iodine and calcium, they showed lesser deficiencies of protein and naicin than whites.[2] These dental and nutritional findings (with the exception of decayed, missing and filled teeth) also follow when low income persons are compared to high. However, in 1968, blacks were three times as likely to have a nutritional deficiency of some type than whites.[1]

Utilization of Services

With these differences in status and need in mind, we now turn to differences in utilization of services. The introduction of Medicaid and Medicare significantly increased the number of visits to a doctor per person per year for the disadvantaged. However,even after these payment mechanisms were available, blacks had fewer visits to both dentists and physicians in 1973 than did whites.[2] The difference is most marked in those under 17 years of age and in low income families.[1]

Also, there were fewer visits to both dentists and physicians for blacks in all income categories. Further differences in utilization of outpatient services are shown in Table 3.3. Note the pattern for increased usage of outpatient clinic, emergency room or public services by blacks in contrast to whites.

In 1973, whites had a higher short stay hospital discharge rate (157.4) than blacks (147.2), but the latter had a higher rate for days of care and thus longer average stays: 8.8 for blacks as against 7.6 for whites.[7]

Preventive care is less frequent in racial minorities but, as might be expected, this is related to family income with the lower income families and minorities less likely to receive such services as a general checkup, measles vaccination, or prenatal care.[2]

In spite of Medicare, when minorities utilized physicians' services they incurred lower expenses than did whites.[1] A smaller percentage of non-white enrollees received Medicare services in all parts of the country, than did whites, the difference being greatest in the South.[1] Reimbursement per person enrolled was also less for non-white persons than white except for hospital outpatient services.[1] Similarly, Medicaid payments per recipient have been less for non-white than white persons and again this difference is noted for all age groups and all regions of the country.[1]

However, Medicare and Medicaid have improved access for the minorities and the poor. As a result these groups have experienced sharper decreases in

TABLE 3.3

Rates Per 1,000 Population for Selected
Outpatient Visits by Race, 1973-74*

	White	Non-white
M.D. & D.O. Offices	3,569.2	2,702.1
Dental Visits	1,717.6	922.9
Hospital Outpatient Clinics	282.7	735.8
Emergency Rooms	177.1	316.2
†Outpatient Psychiatric Departments	2.2	3.9
†Free-standing Psychiatric Clinics	2.4	2.3
Company Clinics	40.2	52.9
Family Planning Clinics (Female)	43.1	170.8
Other Physician Visits (Schools, Health Departments etc.)	213.3	335.6

*Adapted from: The Nation's Use of Health Resources 1976 Edition, Department of Health Education and Welfare, 1977 pp 22, 30, 31, 37, 38, 39.
†1971

the percent who have not had a doctor's visit in the previous two years than have the non-poor and whites.[2] In addition, more facilities now accept minority patients than did formerly.[1]

Summary

In summary, minorities in general at this time have improved health status, increased access to health services, and increased utilization of such services compared to earlier years, but still in general, lag behind the majority of people in the U.S. The right to health care still is not a reality for many people and the final answer to their needs is not solely in the area of financing but involves a number of other factors which must be addressed if further improvement is to be accomplished.

REFERENCES

1. Minority Health Chart Book. Washington, D.C., American Public Health Association, 1974, pp 1, 4, 49, 62, 63, 76-82.
2. Health of the Disadvantaged. US DHEW, Public Health Service, 1977, p 61, 23-41.
3. Socioeconomic Issues of Health, Chicago, IL, AMA, 1979, pp 165, 167.
4. Health Status of Minorities and Low-Income Groups. US DHEW, Public Health Service, 1979, pp 213, 48.
5. Mortality from fires and conflagrations, Metropolitan Life Insurance Co. Statistical Bulletin, 60:4, 1979.

6. Health, United States 1976—1977 Chartbook. US DHEW, Public Health Service, 1977, p 14.
7. The Nation's Use of Health Resources. 1976, US DHEW, Public Health Service, 1977, p 48.

Epidemiology

4

Terence R. Collins, M.D., M.P.H.

Definition

Epidemiology has been defined traditionally as the study of the distribution of disease in human populations; the focus of epidemiology is a population rather than the individual. A shift in the patterns of morbidity and mortality in the western world from acute infectious disease processes to diseases of a chronic nature has changed the role of epidemiology accordingly. Epidemiologists now study not only the distribution of disease, but the multiple variables which affect the outcome both of the disease process and of health care. Thus, epidemiologists are intimately involved in the development of new types of health care delivery. Epidemiology becomes closely associated with the terms community medicine and health services research as the basic methodology is applied to developing procedures for evaluation and cost-benefit analysis. Epidemiology is essential for the planning of community health services. The clinician uses the principles of epidemiology in the process of differential diagnosis and in developing a critical approach to the medical literature.

Measures of Disease Occurrence

Initially epidemiology deals with a description of the distribution of a health problem. Differentiation between a ratio and a rate is important in the study of epidemiologic data. A *ratio* is a relative number expressing the magnitude of one occurrence or condition in relationship to another. A *rate,* on the other hand, is a measure of some event, disease, or condition in relation to a unit of population along with some specification of time. A true rate exists only if the numerator is included as part of the denominator, and if the denominator represents the entire population at risk of developing the condition or experiencing the event. The numerator of a rate is relatively easy to obtain from various health records, vital statistics and health agencies. The denominator is one of the most difficult determinations for which an accurate assessment can be made. In order to include only the population at risk in the denominator, all individuals who have had the condition previously must be excluded. In the application to health services, the population at risk for obtaining services at a specific facility should not be receiving similar services from another health facility. The problems are obvious.

Two rates, used routinely in epidemiologic studies, are frequently confused in clinical medicine. *Incidence* is the number of new cases of a disease divided by the population at risk over a period of time. *Prevalence* is defined as the number of existing cases of a disease divided by the total population at a single point in time. Figure 4.1 illustrates the concept of prevalence.

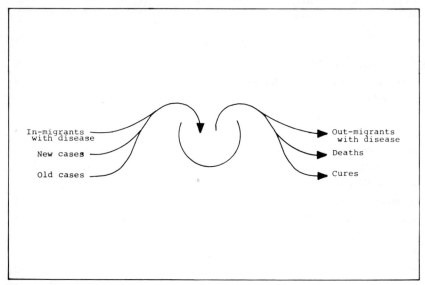

In-migrants with disease

New cases

Old cases

Out-migrants with disease

Deaths

Cures

Fig. 4.1 Prevalence pot

The incidence rate is the critical and fundamental tool for most studies dealing with etiological factors for both acute and chronic illness and these studies can give direct indicators of the risk of disease. High incidence is usually synonymous with high risk of disease. High prevalence, however, does not necessarily signify high risk. It may reflect an increased survival rate due to better medical care or prolonged duration of the disease. Conversely, a low prevalence rate could reflect low incidence, a rapid rate of cure of a disease process, or a rapidly fatal disease process. Because prevalence is observed at a point in time, its use is limited in studies relating to cross sectional observations in which both causes and effects are observed simultaneously.

Prevalence varies with the incidence and duration of disease. If conditions are stable with incidence and duration constant over time, prevalence equals the product of incidence and duration, or $P = I \times D$. Duration would be measured from the same point as the time of incidence, eg, time of diagnosis.

Epidemiology

Table 4.1 illustrates prevalence and incidence of coronary heart disease for various age groups. If only prevalence data were available, it would be assumed that coronary heart disease exists with equal frequency in young adults of both sexes, but in reality the risk is over 20 times higher in males than in females. An explanation for this lies in the different course of the disease between young men and young women. In young men there is a very high incidence of acute myocardial infarction and sudden death, but in women sudden death is much less common and the disease has a longer duration. Prevalence thus could actually be equal in the two sexes despite the greater incidence in males.

TABLE 4.1

Prevalence and Incidence of Coronary Heart Disease in the Framingham Study. Prevalence at Initial Examination. Incidence is over an eight year period in persons free of disease at initial examination*

	Males		Females	
Age	Prevalence Rate/1000	Incidence Rate/1000	Prevalence Rate/1000	Incidence Rate/1000
30-39	5	24	5	1
40-49	38	66	15	10
50-59	48	131	22	67

*Adapted from Mausner & Bahn: Epidemiology: An Introductory Text. 1974, Courtesy W.B. Saunders and Authors.

Prevalence figures are valuable in the area of health planning and for disease control services because they reflect the duration as well as incidence. This information can be useful in monitoring control programs for chronic diseases which have impact on the health care system over time.

When dealing with rates, crude, specific and adjusted rates must be considered. *Crude rates* are summary rates based on actual number of events in a total population in a given period of time. The crude death rate would be the number of deaths among residents in an area in a calendar year divided by the average population in the area in that year. When we speak of *specific death rates* we are referring to a population subgroup and usually are referring to age specific death rates which are defined as follows: the number of deaths among residents of a given age (such as 25 to 34 years) in a calendar year divided by the average population (age 25 to 34 years) in the area in that year times a multiplier, usually 100,000. For example, the crude death rate in the

United States in the year 1976 was 8.9 per 1,000, or 890 per 100,000, while the age specific death rates varied from 1,600 per 100,000 under one year of age, to 150 per 100,000 in the age 25 to 34 age group, to 3,333 per 100,000 in the age 65 to 74 age group.[1]

There is also a need for a third type of rate. The *adjusted rate* is also a summary rate but is based on age specific rate information. The adjusted rate presents a summary figure for the total population. This rate is calculated in such a way as to remove the effect of differences in the distribution of the variable for any specific comparison. Thus, an age adjusted rate, which is the most commonly used adjusted rate, is a rate in which the effects of age on the statistic have been removed. In the calculation of these rates a standard population is selected and compared with other adjusted rates using the same standard population. Any difference found must be due to differences in the age specific rates and not due to the composition of different age groups within each population. It should be noted that adjustment can be used for any variable in which it is desired to remove the effect of that variable on the data being analyzed, if the detailed information on the population is available. The age adjusted death rate for the United States in 1976 was 630 per 100,000 population.[1]

Another commonly used adjusted rate is the *standardized mortality ratio (SMR)* which is defined as the observed deaths over the expected deaths x 100. The SMR is a useful tool for looking at groups of people when details on age specific rates are not available or numbers in specific groups are small. A common use of the SMR is in studies of occupational illness.

The problem of environmental exposure to asbestos illustrates the application of the SMR. In Table 4.2 it can be seen that this group of retired asbestos workers had a slightly greater SMR than the general population in which the observed and expected rate would be in approximately a one-to-one ratio giving an SMR of 100. It can be seen that deaths due to cancer of the respiratory tract significantly exceeded deaths due to this cause in the general population with an SMR of 267.3. Recent research supports the causal relationship between cancer of the respiratory tract and asbestos exposure.

A final concept of disease occurrence is that of the secular trend. Secular trend is a change in disease rates over an extended period of time. Figure 4.2 shows the incidence of reported cases of malaria in the United States from 1933—1977.

Study Design

Observational Epidemiology

Epidemiologic studies are often started by simply describing events. This involves the classic description of who is affected. When and where do the cases occur? Specification of *person, place* and *time* is the first trinity of

TABLE 4.2

Observed and Expected Deaths and SMR's for
Selected Causes of Death for Asbestos Workers: 1969*

| | All Ages | | |
Causes of Death	Observed	Expected	SMR
All causes	754	655.2	115.1
Cancer	167	109.4	152.6
Digestive	53	41.8	126.8
Respiratory	58	21.7	267.3
All other cancer	56	45.9	122.0

*Adapted from Enterline P, Henderson V: Type of asbestos and respiratory cancer in the asbestos industry. Archives of Environmental Health (27:314, November 1973). Courtesy publisher and author. Copyright 1973, American Medical Association.

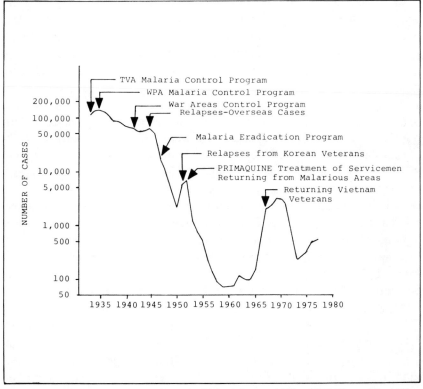

Fig 4.2 Malaria - reported cases by year, United States, 1933—1977 (From Morbidity and Mortality Weekly Report Annual Summary 1977. 26(53):56, 1978).

Terence Collins   31

epidemiology and these provide much of the basis for inquiry. There are many demographic variables to be considered in descriptive studies, the first and probably the most important, being *age*. All mortality and morbidity rates show some relationship to age. The time of life at which an infectious disease predominates is influenced by such factors as the degree of exposure to the agent at different ages, variation in susceptibility with age, and the duration of the immunity developed after infection. This illustrates the second trinity of epidemiology; *agent, host,* and *environment.* Traditionally, these factors were thought of in terms of infectious disease, but now are seen as critical determinants in the study of chronic diseases, especially cancer.

Increasing prevalence with age is characteristic of chronic diseases such as osteoarthritis or diabetes. It should be noted that age marks the passage of time, so that instead of a degenerative disease process, we could be dealing with an infectious problem with a long latent period such as seen in the slow virus diseases. Both Hodgkin's disease and multiple sclerosis have been implicated potentially as having a slow virus etiology.

A second major differential variable in descriptive epidemiology is *sex.* In general, it can be stated that the death rates are higher for males than females, but morbidity rates are generally higher for females. Many characteristics of males and females other than hormones contribute to differential outcomes in health. These include social roles, personality factors, and differing health behaviors.

Ethnic group or race must be considered in describing health in a population. In the 1970 census, the Bureau of the Census classified the population as "white" and "all other". The white population comprised 87.4% of the total and 12.6% of the population fell into the "all other" group. About 90% of the "all other" population represents Negro, to use Census Bureau terminology. A common disease, hypertension, illustrates variation by skin color in that there is a difference in the course of essential hypertension in the black and white populations. In the black population the high blood pressure appears at a younger age, is at higher levels, and is associated with earlier onset of complications, morbidity and mortality. In 1976, the age adjusted death rate for hypertension in white males was 1.8 per 100,000 population, compared to 5.4 per 100,000 population for all other males.[1]

Social class is one method of ranking or stratifying the population into subgroups. There are a variety of different mechanisms to measure social class. The single most commonly used variable to relate income and social class is *occupation*. Occupation in itself is a difficult subject to study because of the fact that an individual may work at different jobs for varying periods of time and, even within the same job, may have differing rates of exposure to a variety of variables ranging from stress, to toxic chemicals, to environmental hazards such as asbestos. *Education* is also used as a proxy measure to estimate social class. The infant mortality rate varies for whites from 30.3 per 1,000 live births with fathers having eight years or less education, to 17.0 for the group with fathers having four years of college education.[2]

There are many problems that have a distinct association with the *place* in which the disease occurs. Looking at various regions within the country, there is the north to south gradient of multiple sclerosis with the disease being more prevalent in the northern latitudes. It is also necessary to look at areas with smaller defined geographic divisions. Different disease prevalence occurs within areas of a large city, often corresponding to the differing distribution by social class. The difference between urban and rural patterns of morbidity and mortality indicates health may be related to the lifestyles of these different regions.

Time is a classic variable in the study of disease processes. Disease patterns show cyclic patterns which may be annual (seasonal) or have some other periodicity. For example, measles epidemics occurred every two to three years prior to widespread immunization practices. Influenza A epidemics tend to occur in two to three year cycles while epidemics of influenza B are more widely spaced, ranging from four to six years. Clustering of cases in time, though often not easily identified, can be very useful in identifying a causal relationship.

An observational method which is commonly in use now is that of the epidemiologic surveillance. The system which receives much attention is the CDC's Influenza Surveillance Reporting System,which includes 121 cities. Over 4,000 surveillance sites are used, consisting of 1,572 schools and industries, 848 sentinal physicians and hospitals, 1,651 county based health units, and 91 laboratories. All of these systematically report morbidity and virus isolation data to state, territorial and military epidemiologists where the information is forwarded to CDC for analysis using a computer-based information system.[3] Using this type of data, epidemics can be defined, as illustrated in Figure 4.3. This is the standard method by which an epidemic curve is shown to exceed a previously calculated threshold level. The threshold level indicates variation that can normally be expected. This graph illustrates the seasonal character of influenza related mortality and the spacing of the epidemics from 1973 to 1975.

To summarize, descriptive or observational studies are used basically, to collect, aggregate, and analyze data in preparation for development of a future hypothesis or possibly intervention.

Retrospective Studies

Once the descriptive observations have been collected and a hypothesis developed, the hypothesis must be evaluated by other studies. Frequently the

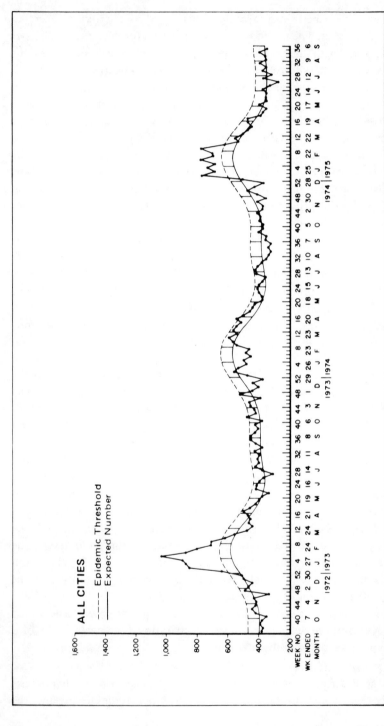

Fig 4.3. Pneumonia-influenza reported deaths in 121 selected cities, by week, United States, 1972—73, 1974—75 (From Morbidity and Mortality Weekly Report Annual Supplement Summary 1975. 24(54):50, 1976.)

Epidemiology

initial studies are *retrospective,* that is, looking into the past for information. These are primarily of two types, *prevalence* and *case control* studies.

Prevalence or cross-sectional studies may be done by field survey or in a cross-sectional manner by looking at data available in records at a single point in time. Prevalence studies are helpful in determining the size of a health problem. Prevalence studies are also often surveys performed on a sampling basis on a large population or on total communities. The data gathered are unlikely to be of great value in testing a hypothesis, but often complement descriptive data and facilitate the design of future studies.

Data tabulation in a prevalence study subdivides the population according to suspected predisposing factors and compares the disease prevalence in each subgroup. For example, when looking at smoking in relation to chronic bronchitis, the group may be divided into various smoking categories. The prevalence of chronic bronchitis in each smoking category is then compared. When interpreting the results of a prevalence study, care must be taken to avoid assigning an unsubstantiated time sequence to an association between a trait or other factor and the disease because these data reflect conditions at a single point in time.

Case control studies are related to prevalence or cross-sectional studies, but because they frequently involve fewer cases, they are more easily conducted. Among the analytical studies, case control studies are often the first approach in determining whether a specific variable is related to disease occurrence.

The initial step in a study of this type is the correct identification of cases. The term "case" need not refer to a diseased state, but only reflect the condition under study. Criteria must be set up to insure that only the cases of interest will be included. Cases may be found in the community, but more often are identified in a hospital, school, or similar population group. The case group will consist of those individuals identified over a defined time period. Controls may be selected in many ways. Detailed discussions of this topic may be found in the bibliographic references. Data is gathered from both cases and controls on demographic, environmental, economic, or other variables of interest, and the relative frequency of the outcome measure is compared.

Ideally, when selecting cases and controls there should be no major differences between the two groups except the factor being studied. This is not totally possible in a human population, but striving to achieve this is the goal of good study design. One concept that is important is the goal of good study design. One concept that is important to consider in selection of controls is that of *matching.* By matching the case and the control on a particular characteristic, the difference in this characteristic as a possible contributor to the overall difference between the two groups is eliminated. In the study relating smoking to chronic bronchitis, when age was matched and the subsequent finding showed a difference in the prevalence of chronic bronchitis, then age could not be the explanation for this difference. Matching is usually limited to a few variables in order to simplify the procedure of obtaining an appropriate number of controls. In many case controlled studies, multiple controls for each case may be used in order to increase the validity of the conclusion.

In case control studies, the results are expressed as the relative frequency of the variable or characteristic in the diseased versus the non-diseased categories. This may be illustrated graphically in Figure 4.4, commonly called a 2 by 2 table. A useful way to look at this data is to calculate the *relative risk*. The relative risk is defined as the ratio of the rate of those exposed to a factor to the rate of those not exposed. Using the letters in Figure 4.4, the relative risk would be calcualted as: $\frac{a}{a+b} \div \frac{c}{c+d}$. An estimate of the relative risk may be obtained by using a simpler formula, derived from the table: $\frac{ad}{bc}$. Relative risk can be estimated from a retrospective study if it is assumed that the controls are representative of the general population, the cases are representative of all cases, and the frequency of the disease in the population is small.

Causal associations cannot be defined in a retrospective study. The identified associations may suggest a cause and effect relationship, but a prospective study must confirm this relationship. If a series of retrospective studies give a consistently high relative risk, the possibility of causal association becomes much stronger. This, in fact, has been the case in the arguments concerning the etiological relationship between smoking and lung cancer where actual biological proof linking the two in the human being has not been developed. Retrospective studies with consistently high relative risks strengthen the assertion that smoking causes lung cancer.

		OUTCOME (DISEASE)		
		Present	Absent	Total
E X P	With	a	b	a + b
O S U R E	Without	c	d	c + d
	Total	a + c	b + d	a + b + c + d = N

Fig 4.4 Illustration of a 2 x 2 table

Prospective studies

Prospective Studies include individuals without the disease or outcome at the beginning of the study period and proceed to follow them through time. *Cohort study* is a term also describing prospective studies when a cohort or identifiable group is followed over time and observed for the development of the disease or outcome. Thus, when speaking of prospective studies, we are speaking of incidence studies. The cohort may be a general population group such as residents of a specific area, or a more specialized population such as an occupational group or a group of insured individuals. The cohort may be selected because of a previously known exposure to a suspected causative factor. A classic example of this selection process is the observation of a cohort of Japanese that were exposed to the atomic bomb explosions. These populations have been followed and noted to have developed various types of cancer. The great importance of cohort or incidence studies is that they provide a direct measurement of risk.

Because of the time and expense involved, a serious decision must be made before carrying on this type of study and an extensive planning period is required. The duration of follow-up necessary in a prospective study is determined primarily by the number of cases needed to provide a reliable statistically significant answer to the specific questions under study. Some consideration must be given to the natural history of the condition studied so that a long latent period may be identified.

Analysis of data in a prospective study is complicated. The use of *person-years* of observation is the standard method for handling variable follow-up periods. If the population is involved in the study for differing periods of time the denominator of the incidence rate is then expressed in person-months, days, or years, whichever is most appropriate. Using this approach each subject contributes only the time of actual observation to the population at risk. If the subject leaves after one year he contributes one person-year, or if after ten, ten person-years, etc. A basic assumption in the use of person-years is that the disease risk remains relatively constant over time. This is a significant assumption in the study of chronic disease and must be constantly re-evaluated.

In the analysis of data from a cohort study, the relative risk is calculated in a similar manner to case control studies. The numerator is now incidence in the exposed and the denominator is incidence in the non-exposed. *Attributable risk* is defined as the rate of the disease in exposed individuals that can be attributed to the specific exposure. It is derived by subtracting the incidence of the disease among non-exposed persons from the corresponding rate among exposed persons. Using attributable risk we could study the impact of smoking on the development of chronic bronchitis in a population.

Attributable risk gives a number which estimates the impact of exposure on the population. This is of great interest for health services administration and planning. In contrast, the importance of relative risk is that it approximates the strength of etiologic relationship and is of more interest to the researcher or to the individuals developing an intervention strategy. Attributable risk is a rate while relative risk is a ratio.

Different attributable risks for lung cancer and coronary heart disease can be compared as seen in Table 4.3. In this example there is a high relative risk for heavy smokers as compared to non-smokers suggesting a strong association between smoking and lung cancer. The relative risk for coronary heart disease for heavy smokers is much smaller; that is, 1.4. This suggests that if coronary heart disease is to be prevented, other factors than smoking must be considered as part of the intervention process. Because the deaths from coronary heart disease are so common among the non-exposed, even a fairly small increase in the rate attributable to smoking can create an absolute increase in death rate that is as large as for lung cancer. In comparing the attributable risks of 177/100,000 for coronary heart disease and 159/100,000 for lung cancer valuable information is developed for planning future health facility needs.

Interpretation of prospective studies must focus not only on the prediction of disease occurrence, but on how this relates to individual risk and cause and effect. The classic prospective study is the Framingham Study. This is a long-term study aimed at evaluating the health of an entire community in

TABLE 4.3

Comparison of Relative Risk and Attributable Risk in Mortality From Lung Cancer and From Coronary Heart Disease for Heavy Smokers and Nonsmokers (Data from Doll and Hill[4])

Exposure Category	Annual Death Rates Per 100,000 Persons	
	Lung Cancer	Coronary Heart Disease
Heavy smokers	166	599
Nonsmokers	7	422
Measure of Excess Risk		
Relative risk:	$\frac{166}{7} = 23.7$	$\frac{599}{422} = 1.4$
Attributable risk:	166 – 7 = 159	599 – 422 = 177

Massachusetts and specifically focusing on cardiovascular disease. The study began in 1950. It was planned to last at least 20 years because of the hypothesized slow development of atherosclerosis and its consequences. This study has provided the core of information on the natural history of many chronic diseases.

The choice between performing a retrospective or prospective study is based on evaluation of many variables. These would include time, expense, ease of obtaining information and potential sources of bias.

Experimental Studies

Experimental studies resemble incidence studies in that follow-up of the subjects is necessary to determine outcome. However, the essential distinguishing feature of experiments is that they involve some intervention or change in the process on the part of the investigators. The method is to divide the study population into two groups, then provide the treatment or exposure to or removal of a particular exposure under investigation from one group and not the other. The groups are then followed for the development or absence of disease. This method is considered to be the best test of the cause and effect hypothesis. Random assignment to experimental or control group is the preferred method. Two examples of experimental studies that have been used are the vaccine trial and the clinical trial.

The vaccine trial, of which the poliomyelitis trial is the best known, has made a great contribution to the improvement of health worldwide. Unfortunately, because of ethical problems which will be discussed later, we may have seen the last of the great vaccine trials. Figure 4.5 illustrates the annual incidence rates of polio in the United States from 1935 to 1965. It should be noted that there was a sharp drop in the incidence of polio prior to the onset of vaccines. It is not clearly established from this information whether the addition of the inactivated vaccine to our health care system influenced the curve directly. A controlled study was performed in the United States to test oral polio vaccines and the results revealed that 28 cases per 100,000 population developed in those given vaccine versus 71 per 100,000 in those given placebo. The protection appeared to be only against paralytic poliomyelitis since there were no appreciable differences between vaccinated and controls in the incidence of non-paralytic disease.[5]

In all experimental studies, significant ethical problems are encountered by providing a treatment or therapeutic modality which may be beneficial and then deliberately denying it to some members of the study group. The investigator must have an idea that the treatment has an excellent chance of helping the patient. On the other hand, there should be significant doubt about the value of what is presently being done compared to what is to be done experimentally. There is also a difficulty regarding the confidentiality of

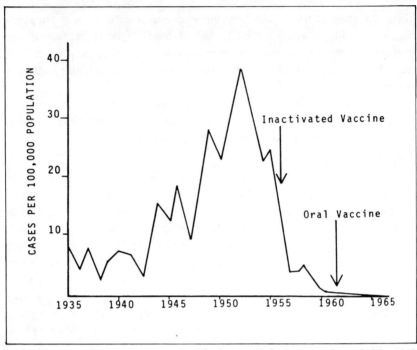

Fig 4.5. Annual incidence rates of polio in the United States from 1935—1965 (Adapted from Morris L et al: Surveillance of poliomyelitis in the U.S., 1962—65. Public Health Reports 82:417, 1967.)

records. For the most part, the observational epidemiologist is a passive observer and confidentiality has not been a problem. But in this present era of computerized medical records, the problems of confidentiality and the protection of individual rights in medical records are potentially significant barriers to epidemiologic research. The linkage of one computer back to another creates a potential for serious breaches of confidentiality.

It was not until 1962 that the amendments to the Federal Drug and Cosmetic Act of 1938 made it mandatory to test the efficacy of drugs. This led to a significant increase in the number of clinical trials performed on a variety of existing and new drug preparations. All drugs introduced during this period have not been subjected to careful clinical trials to evaluate their effectiveness and dangers. The question is, really, not whether experimental trials with human subjects are needed, but rather how they should be conducted.

Experiments involve comparisons among several groups. The key issue is the randomization process. Often the randomization cannot be perfect, but it is the goal of studies to randomly allocate to each group. A second important concept commonly referred to is that of blindness. This term may refer to the

Epidemiology

concept that experimental subjects should be kept unaware of whether they are included in the treatment group or in the placebo group. More importantly, the assessment of outcome should be blind. Frequently the term double-blind is encountered. Some authors use this term to refer to experiments where both the assignment to treatment or control group and the assessment of results are blind. Another use refers to experiments in which neither the patient nor the physician knows whether the patient is in the experimental or the control group.

Screening

The concept of *screening* is becoming increasingly important in medicine as prevention receives more attention. Objectives and criteria of screening which should be satisfied can be seen in Figure 4.6. Usually one or more are not satisfied.

In the natural history of disease there are points at which screening must occur if outcome is to be modified. This critical point is indicated by X in Figure 4.7 and is different for each disease. If intervention occurs shortly after point X, the time between diagnosis and outcome may be longer than usually seen; however, the duration of the disease process is not shortened. The period of observation is simply greater. Current controversy exists over this exact

---

OBJECTIVES

1. Improve the health of person screened.

2. Obtain epidemiologic data on diseases, especially natural history.

3. Perfect screening procedures for future use.

4. Obtain baseline data for future medical evaluation.

5. Provide implied benefit to patient.

CRITERIA

1. Disease must have an effect on quality or quantity of life.

2. Acceptable, effective methods of treatment must be available.

3. Detection will significantly affect outcome.

4. Treatment in asymptomatic phase must yield a therapeutic result superior to treatment after appearance of symptom.

5. The screening test should be relatively inexpensive.

6. The screening test should be valid.

7. The natural history of the condition should be known.

8. Disease should have a significant incidence in the population.

9. Policy on who to treat as patients should be agreed upon.

10. Cost effective procedures should be established.

11. Case finding should be a continuing process.

Fig 4.6. Screening

Terence Collins

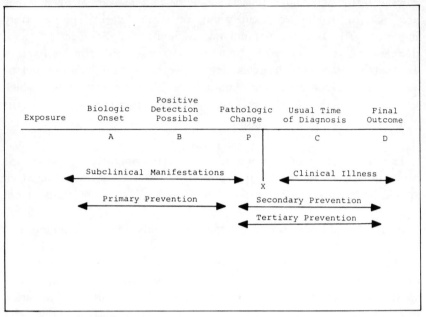

Fig. 4.7. Natural history of disease

issue in cancer therapy. Intervention to the left of X will change the course of the disease and if the total duration is shortened, morbidity and/or mortality should be less. In the case of rabies, X is at point A because of the almost universal fatal outcome of the disease process. In coronary heart disease, there are probably two critical points. The first is before biologic onset reflecting the effects of intervention as far as reduction of tobacco smoking, risk factors screening, modification of risk factors, etc. A second critical point probably occurs fairly close to the point of usual diagnosis, point C. Prevention at this time is by recognition of early warning signs.

Primary prevention is initiated before pathologic change occurs, while *secondary prevention* is defined as coming after this change. *Tertiary prevention* refers to rehabilitation and prevention of disability. The screening modality is governed by the type of prevention that is considered appropriate.

The concepts of *sensitivity* and *specificity* are critical to the determination of the screening level.

Sensitivity represents the proportion of truly diseased who are called diseased by the test. (Diseased persons with a positive test divided by all persons in the population with disease.)

Specificity represents the proportion of truly non-diseased who are so identified by the test. (Non-diseased persons with a negative test divided by all persons in the population without disease.)

Epidemiology

Selection of the screening level will be based on the estimated prevalence of the disease. Often the high risk group will be screened to increase the cost effectiveness of the procedure. The next step will be to estimate the number of persons to be screened. After evaluation of the sensitivity and specificity of the test and after opportunities to rescreen or diagnose the cases studied, it is necessary to consider inconveniences or dangers of the diagnostic examination.

Prediction of risk cannot be done from the sensitivity alone. If prediction is from positivity of a test, then the prevalence of the condition in the population must be known. This combination of sensitivity and prevalence can be used to calculate the predictive value. The method of calculation can be found in formulas available in many textbooks of epidemiology, such as Mausner and Bahn's *Epidemiology: An Introductory Text.*

There are also certain risks to screening. There may be damage due to the labeling of patients by false positives, such as a false positive VDRL which can cause great embarrassment and potential long term harm to an individual. The second risk is that the reason for screening is subverted if services to identify and treat the process are not available. The Early Periodic Screening, Diagnosis, and Treatment program of Medicaid has demonstrated this problem. Screening generally should be integrated with the medical care program where treatment is to be carried out, and not at peripheral sites where it is anticipated that the individual with an abnormal reading will obtain verification and appropriate treatment but no follow-up is carried out.

This has been a very brief introduction to the process of screening. A thorough understanding of the epidemiologic principals behind screening is necessary for a clinician to make adequate decisions as to what screening tests will be used in the particular practice and at what levels determinations of illness or pathology will be made.

REFERENCES

1. Final Mortality Statistics 1976. Monthly Vital Statistics Report. 26(12) Supp (2), 1978.
2. Infant Mortality Rates: Socioeconomic Factors. US DHEW. Public Health Service, National Center for Health Statistics. Ser 22, No 14, 1972.
3. Influenza Surveillance Reporting System, 1976—77. Morbidity and Mortality Weekly Report 26:291, 1977.
4. Doll, R Hill AB: Lung cancer and other causes of death in relation to smoking. Br Med J 2:1071—1081, 1956.
5. Frances E et al: An evaluation of the 1954 poliomyelitis vaccine trials: summary report. A J Public Health, Vol 45, (5), part 2, 1955.

BIBLIOGRAPHY

Alderson M: An Introduction to Epidemiology. Massachusetts, PSG Publishing Co, Inc, 1977.

Terence Collins

Friedman G: Primer of Epidemiology. New York, NY, McGraw-Hill Inc, 1974.

Lilienfeld A: Foundations of Epidemiology. New York, NY, Oxford Community Press, 1976.

MacMahon, Pugh, TF: Epidemiology Principles and Methods. Boston, MA, Little, Brown and Co, 1970.

Mauser J, Bahn A: Epidemiology: An Introductory Text. Philadelphia, PA, W B Saunders Co, 1974.

Biostatistics

5

James D. Leeper, Ph.D.

Biostatistics is the application of statistical concepts and techniques to the design of experiments, collection and processing of data, analysis of data, and interpretation of results from data arising from the biological and medical/ health sciences. These techniques are so numerous and varied as to degree of difficulty that it is impossible to discuss all of them here. The purpose of this chapter is to help explain some basic statistical concepts and to introduce some elementary statistical procedures. It is emphasized that the researcher should consult a statistician before, during, and after the collection of data. The proper planning and implementation of a study from a statistical point of view allows precise statements to be made about the results in terms of probabilility.

Basic Concepts

We are all familiar with everyday usage of words such as population, sample, statistics, variability and probability. The strict mathematical definitions of these terms are sometimes ominous, but the meanings are quite close to what one might suspect. These words represent basic concepts in statistics and will now be reviewed.

First, a definition of statistics is in order. *Statistics* may be defined as the science of collecting, analyzing and interpreting data obtained from a group of experimental units. Notice that this definition includes more than just the mathematical calculations involved in the analysis phase. Equally important is the planning necessary for proper collection of data and the interpretation of the results. A distinction needs to be made between statistics, which is a field of study, and a statistic, which is any quantity that may be computed from a set of data.

Conventionally, the field of statistics is broken into two parts. The topic of *descriptive statistics* is concerned with techniques for organizing, summarizing and communicating data. *Inferential statistics* refers to methodologies for estimating quantities and in testing hypotheses about populations by using sample data. These two topics will be discussed later.

When we hear the word "population", we usually think of the number of people in a nation, state, county, or city. These are examples of populations in the statistical sense. In general, a *population* is a group of all objects which have some characteristics in common. Therefore, a population is whatever it is defined to be, but it must be defined precisely as to what characteristics the individuals in this population have in common. For example, a population could be defined to be all females between the ages of 45 and 64 who resided in Alabama on September 1, 1978, who were eligible for Medicaid.

We usually think of a sample as being a small part of some whole quantity. Statistically, a *sample* is a part of some defined population. Just as no two people or objects are exactly alike, the same thing can be said about any two groups or samples of people or objects. This leads to the concept of *variability* and *sampling variation*. There is almost always some inherent variability among individuals in populations and samples. There is also variability among repeated samples from the same population, ie, sampling variation. All of inferential statistics is based on examining the variability observed in a sample and relating it to other quantities.

Everyday, we deal with probability, at least on a subjective level. *Probability* may be seen as the chance of something happening. When you are sitting in your car contemplating making a left turn and a truck is coming toward you, your mind is calculating the probability of surviving if you attempt the turn. Unfortunately, sometimes these subjective calculations are incorrect. The probability of an event occurring may also be thought of as the relative frequency or proportion of times it will occur out of all possible times that it *may* occur. For example, if a large number of coal miners are screened for black lung disease, then the observed proportion of them having the disease is an estimate of the probability that a miner will contract this disease.

Sampling Techniques

When investigating a certain characteristic (or variable) in a population, the most intuitively appealing procedure is to obtain information about everyone. Such a procedure is called a *census*. The most well-known census is, of course, the one conducted by the U.S. Bureau of the Census every tenth year. *Vital statistics* also consist of data concerning all vital events (eg, births, deaths) that occur in a population. Clearly, it is impossible for every researcher to conduct a census of whatever population he or she defines every time a study is to be conducted. Therefore, the idea of investigating a *sample* of the population is essential.

Sampling, however, has the disadvantage of providing incomplete information about a population. Sampling is necessary though, and compared to a census, has the advantages of reduced cost, greater speed, greater flexibility in the type of information that can be obtained, and greater accuracy in the data since those obtaining and processing it may be more highly trained and more carefully supervised. The reduced cost and increased speed in data collection, processing and analysis result from the smaller number of subjects and decreased amount of data. One example of greater flexibility is that a researcher may consider drawing blood from a small sample, but would not conceive of attempting it from everyone in a very large population.

Probability sampling, which means the probability or chance of any individual being in the sample is known prior to sampling, provides the best sampling techniques. These techniques include simple random, stratified, systematic and cluster sampling

In *simple random sampling,* each possible sample of a population has an equal chance of being chosen. Tables of random numbers are used to select a simple random sample. In *stratified sampling* the population is first divided into subpopulations called strata and then a separate sample is selected within each stratum. The strata are defined according to known characteristics of the population such as age, race, sex or size of institution. Stratified sampling is used if data of known precision are wanted for certain subpopulations, if sampling problems differ extensively in different subpopulations, to get more precise information, or for administrative convenience. *Systematic sampling* may be used when the sampling units are listed in a file or record book or appear at a central location over a period of time. Then a starting point is chosen at random from a table of random numbers and every k^{th} individual after that point is included in the sample. The value of k depends on the desired sample size and the population size. *Cluster sampling* involves grouping individuals together into clusters who are close in space and/or time. Then clusters are chosen at random and individuals chosen at random within the selected clusters. Cluster sampling is especially useful when sampling a large area.

Non-probablistic or convenience sampling is tempting, but it is almost impossible to make inferences about a larger population from such sample results. This type of sampling typically involves choosing a convenient group of individuals such as one's classmates or neighbors to be in the sample. Even if the researcher is careful to be sure the distribution of certain characteristics in the sample match those of the population, other biases usually enter into the selection.

Even if a sample is properly drawn, the results will most likely differ to some extent from the true situation for the whole population. Some of the error is due to sampling variation, ie, no two samples are exactly alike. Other sources of error are failure to measure some of the chosen sampling units (nonresponse), errors of measurement, and errors of editing, coding, and tabulating of the data. Note that a census is prone to these last three sources of error also, perhaps even more so than a sample.

One popular type of study that involves sampling is the *sample survey*. The basic steps of a sample survey are:

1) Prepare a clear statement of the objectives of the survey.
2) Define the population to be sampled (the target population).
3) Verify that the data to be collected are relevant to the objectives of the survey.
4) Specify the degree of accuracy wanted in the results. This helps determine the sample size that is desirable.
5) Choose the measuring instrument (eg, self-administered questionnaire, interviewer, physical examination) and the method of approaching the population (eg, by mail, telephone, personal visit). Questionnaire and form construction are very important.
6) Divide the population into sampling units (eg, individuals, households) and construct a comprehensive list of sampling units.
7) Select the sample.
8) Try out the measuring instrument and method on a small scale in order to determine its validity and reliability and make revisions as needed.
9) Organize administrative aspects such as training of personnel, managing of data, and checking quality of data.
10) Summarize and analyze the data.
11) Record information on costs, problems, and mistakes for reference when planning new studies.

There are numerous correct ways of carrying out many of these steps. Each method has particular advantages and disadvantages and circumstances when it is most appropriate. Most of the steps are interrelated and if any one is done haphazardly, it will affect others. In order to draw inferences about the population based on what is observed in the sample, proper sampling procedures must be observed and valid measuring instruments must be used. This is a good time to consult a statistician, if one has not already. The basic idea is to select a sample so that it is representative of the population on the average. If the sample does not have this property, then it is called *biased*.

Descriptive Statistics

After data have been collected either from a census or sample, they need to be organized and summarized to help understand their impact and to communicate them to others. Organization of data usually involves the construction of tables and graphs. The researcher needs to make a judgment as to what is the best method to suit the purposes of the study and the type of data collected, preferably before collecting the data.

Table construction should follow certain general principles which are:

1) Tables should be as simple as possible. Including too much in one table is confusing.

2) Tables should be self-explanatory. Everything in the table should be clearly and concisely labeled and defined. Totals and units of measurement should be given.
3) The source of the data should be given if the data are not original.

From the data in Table 5.1, one may illustrate the racial make-up of Northern and Western Alabama counties. One way of accomplishing this is to construct a table of the frequency distribution of this data. A *frequency distribution* shows how often each value of some variable occurs. A *relative frequency distribution* shows what proportion of the total number of measurements occurs at each of the values of the variable. This may be computed from the frequency distribution by dividing each frequency by the total number of observations. A *cumulative relative frequency distribution* is calculated by accumulating or adding together successive relative frequencies. It shows what proportion of the total number of measurements occurs at or below each of the values of the variable. The grouped frequency, relative

TABLE 5.1

Percentage of Non-Whites and Median Family Incomes for
19 Northern and Western Alabama Counties
(U.S. Census Bureau Report, 1970)

County	Percentage of Non-whites	Median Family Income
Bibb	27.9	$5,600
Colbert	36.2	7,700
Cullman	1.0	6,200
Fayette	13.9	5,500
Franklin	5.0	6,000
Greene	75.4	3,000
Hale	66.4	3,900
Jackson	5.2	6,400
Lamar	13.7	5,200
Lauderdale	10.6	7,600
Lawrence	18.8	6,100
Limestone	17.2	6,800
Madison	15.4	10,400
Marion	2.9	6,000
Marshall	2.2	6,600
Morgan	9.4	8,400
Pickens	41.7	5,300
Tuscaloosa	24.3	7,400
Winston	0.4	6,300

frequency, and cumulative relative frequency distributions are illustrated in Table 5.2. The frequencies are shown for a range of values of the variables in this case. Grouping is desirable if there are a large number of values of the variable compared to the total number of measurements. Note that the category boundaries (range of values) for the groups should not overlap.

Another way of illustrating this data is by means of graph techniques. The same general rules as stated for tables also pertain to graphs. A graph is a method of showing quantitative data using a coordinate system. No more coordinate lines than necessary as a guide should be used. Lines of the graph should be heavier than the coordinate lines. The frequency is usually represented on the vertical scale and the values of the variable measured on the horizontal scale. Scale divisions should be clearly indicated.

One type of graph commonly used is the *histogram*. This consists of rectangles centered on the values of the variable measured. The height of the rectangle represents the frequency of the value. Figure 5.1 is an example of a histogram which corresponds to the frequency distribution in Table 5.2.

Another type of graph is the *frequency polygon*. This is constructed by connecting, with a straight line, the points which represent the frequencies above the variable values. For grouped distributions, the points above the midpoints of the intervals are connected. An example of a frequency polygon for the grouped distribution of Table 5.2 is shown in Figure 5.2.

A *scatter diagram* is a type of graph which is useful in illustrating the relationship or association between two variables. Sets of paired data are plotted as points on a coordinate system. If the scatter of points shows some pattern, then there may be a relationship between the two variables. Figure 5.3 is a scatter diagram of percent non-white versus median family income from

TABLE 5.2

Percentage of Non-whites in 19 Northern
and Western Alabama Counties
(U.S. Census Bureau Report, 1970)

Percentage of Non-whites	Frequency	Relative Frequency	Cumulative Relative Frequency
0 - 9.9	7	.37	.37
10.0 - 19.9	6	.32	.69
20.0 - 29.9	2	.11	.80
30.0 - 39.9	1	.05	.85
40.0 - 49.9	1	.05	.90
50.0 - 59.9	0	.00	.90
60.0 - 69.9	1	.05	.95
70.0 - 79.9	1	.05	1.00

Biostatistics

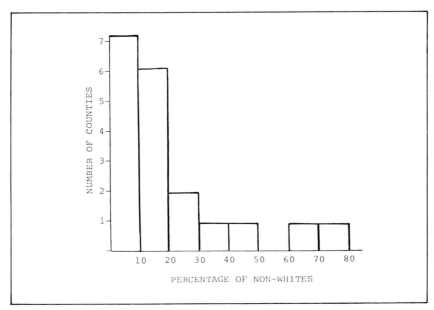

Fig. 5.1. Percentage of non-whites in 19 northern and western Alabama counties (U.S. Census Bureau report, 1970).

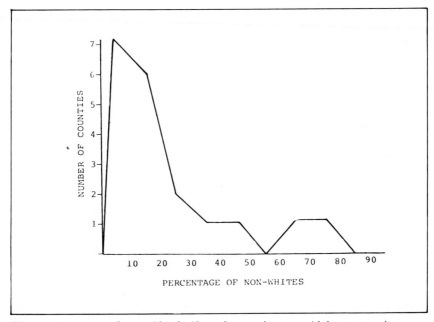

Fig. 5.2. Percentage of non-whites in 19 northern and western Alabama counties (U.S. Census Bureau report, 1970)

James Leeper   51

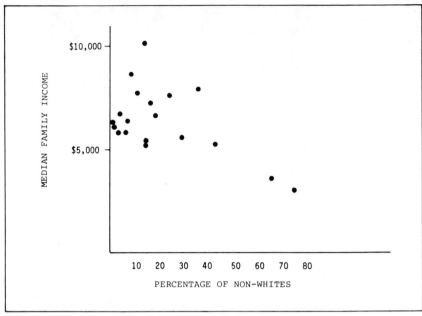

Fig. 5.3. Percentage of non-whites vs. median family income in 19 northern and western Alabama counties (U.S. Census Bureau report, 1970)

Table 5.1. There appears to be a moderate relationship between the two variables. Caution must be taken in inferring causal relationships from such data.

Rules for designing and using tables and graphs may be summarized as follows:

1) Choose the method of presentation which is most effective for your data and purpose.
2) Illustrate one idea at a time.
3) Titles should answer "what, where, and when" to completely identify the data.
4) Labels should be clear and concise.
5) Symbols and codes should be defined.
6) Indicate the source of data if it is not original.
7) Do not manipulate these descriptive tools to imply conclusions that are not supported by the original data.

Data may be summarized in other ways by calculating various statistics from them. Two purposes of summarization are to give an idea of what a typical value is and to describe how spread out the values are. Statistics for describing typical values are called measures of central tendency. Statistics for describing spread are called measures of dispersion or measures of variability.

Three *measures of central tendency* will be discussed here. The *mean* is the arithmetic average of the data. This is calculated by adding the values together and dividing by the number of values. As examples, the mean percentage of non-whites in the example is 20.4 and the mean median family income is $6,300. These are calculated by adding the values together and dividing by 19.

The *mode* of a set of data is the value which occurs most often. Therefore, the modal median family income is $6,000 since it occurs most frequently in the example. There is no modal percentage of non-whites in this example. The mode is not of much value for such a small set of data.

To calculate the *median,* the values must first be ordered from smallest to largest. If the number of values is odd, then the median is the middle value of the ordered array of values. If the number of values is even, then the median is halfway between the two most central values in the ordered array. The median percentage of non-whites is 13.9 and the median median family income is $6,200. Notice that the mean and median percentage of non-whites differ considerably because of the few large values.

The choice of a measure of central tendency depends on the nature of the data being summarized. Each measure has its advantages and disadvantages. The mode is the easiest to compute and is typical in the sense that it is the value that occurs most frequently. Only the mode can be used with the non-numerical data. Sometimes, as with the data in the above example, no one value is much more frequent than several others and the mode may be misleading. In other situations several values may occur with equal frequency, in which case there is no one mode.

For symmetrical distributions the mean and median will be the same. This is not true for a distribution which is not symmetric, ie, a distribution which has more extremely high values than extremely low values or vice versa. The mean is very sensitive to extreme values and gives a distorted sense of what the typical value is. The median is much better in this situation. As an example, this is the reason that median family income is reported in the census rather than mean family income. The mean income is inflated by the few individuals who make a lot of money. Therefore, mean income is not a typical figure whereas median income is not influenced by these large values. Statisticians often prefer the mean because it has certain mathematical properties that are useful in inferential statistics.

The measures of dispersion which are most often used are *variance* and *standard deviation.* One way of calculating the variance is to first compute the mean, subtract the mean from each value, square these differences, add them together, and divide by one less than the number of values. Thus it can be seen that the farther away from the mean the values are, ie, the more spread out the values are, the larger the variance is. The standard deviation is the square root of the variance. For example, the standard deviation for median family income is $1,609 for the 19 Northern and Western Alabama counties.

James Leeper

There is a basic theorem in statistics which says that if an experiment or sampling procedure is repeated many times and a mean of the data is calculated each time, then the frequency distribution of these means tends to take on a certain form. This distribution is symmetrical and bell-shaped and is called the normal or *Gaussian* distribution. This is true even if the frequency distribution of the characteristic itself is very non-normal. For this reason, the normal distribution is very important in statistics even though few, if any, human characteristics are normally distributed. The mean of a particular sample is an estimate of the mean of this distribution. The standard deviation of a particular sample divided by the square root of the sample size is an estimate of the standard deviation of the distribution of means. This standard deviation of means is called the *standard error.*

The normal distribution has a special property. If two times the standard error is added to the mean to obtain one number and subtracted from the mean to obtain another number, then approximately 95% of sample means are between these two numbers. This is true for the normal distribution. It is not true for the mean plus and minus two standard deviations of a non-normal distribution. This fact is often misunderstood, resulting in the misuse of standard deviations. For non-normal distributions, percentiles should be used rather than standard deviation.

Inferential Statistics

The topic of inferential statistics is concerned with estimation and testing hypotheses and arriving at conclusions which extend beyond the immediate sample data. That is, the sample data are used to infer things about the population. There are many methods for doing this, all of which depend on the proper design and execution of the study. Unless one obtains a substantially better knowledge of statistics than what is presented in this chapter, a statistician should be consulted concerning the design, execution and analysis phases of a study.

A *statistical hypothesis* is a statement about a population, not about the sample. It refers to a situation that might be true in the population. The steps for testing a statistical hypothesis are as follows:

1) State the null hyophthesis to be tested along with an alternative hypothesis. The *null hypothesis* is a statement of no differences, either among groups or from what is supposed to be true or has been true in the past. The *alternative hypothesis* is that there is some difference.
2) Choose the design of the experiment or the sampling method.
3) Decide the risk you are willing to take to call the null hypothesis false when actually it is true. This decision determines how large a value the test statistic must have before you will reject the null hypothesis in favor of the alternative hypothesis.

4) Conduct the study and compute the test statistic. If the test statistic is large enough to reject the null hypothesis with the stated level of risk of being wrong, then the result is said to be *statistically significant* at that level of risk.

For example, suppose it is hypothesized or conjectured that family medicine residents in Alabama are more likely to set up a rural practice than family medicine residents in New York. The null hypothesis is that Alabama and New York family medicine residents are equally likely to locate in a rural area. The alternative hypothesis is that the likelihoods of setting up a rural practice are not equal. The study design could be to randomly select 25 Alabama and 25 New York former family medicine residents who have gone on to set up a practice. It is then determined how many are located in rural areas. Suppose it is observed that 32% of the Alabama residents and 20% of the New York residents in the sample are practicing in rural areas. The question now is, "How likely is it that a difference this large or larger would be observed in a sample of this size if there really is no difference in the whole population of former family medicine residents in Alabama and New York?" In other words, how likely is it that this result could be observed by chance due to sampling variation if there really is no difference between the two groups? Suppose it is decided that a 5% risk of incorrectly rejecting the null hypothesis is acceptable. That is, the significance level is chosen to be .05. For the example, an appropriate test finds that the observed difference is not significant at the .05 level. The probability of observing this result by chance— if there really is no difference—is 0.33. Therefore, it is concluded that there is insufficient evidence to reject the null hypothesis that Alabama and New York family medicine residents are equally likely to practice in a rural area. The particular statistical techniques used to test this hypothesis will not be discussed here.

The *significance level* of the test is the stated level of risk of rejecting a true null hypothesis. The conventional significance level that is often used is .05. This means there is a 5% chance of rejecting the null hypothesis when actually it is true and should not be rejected.

As an alternative to stating a significance level, many investigators prefer to report a *p-value*. A p-value is the probability of observing a particular value of the test statistic when the null hypothesis is actually true. Therefore, a small p-value leads one to reject the null hypothesis because the probability or chance that it is true is small.

A distinction must be drawn between statistical significance and *practical significance*. Statistical significance pertains to the reality of an effect, but not to its magnitude. Practical significance is judged by considering the estimated magnitude in light of the investigator's medical or health knowledge. The difference in the outcome of two treatments, for example, may be statistically significant, but the magnitude of the difference may not be practically or clinically significant.

The failure to obtain a statistically significant result does not prove that no real effect exists. Such a failure may be due to a variety of reasons; some are sample size, large population variability, or small real differences.

It has become increasingly easy to perform statistical analyses to test hypotheses. This results from the wide dissemination of computer program packages designed for this purpose. These packages are invaluable tools, but they also open the door for misuse. Computer scientists warn that if you put garbage into a computer, you get garbage out. It is easy to dump a lot of numbers into a computer and obtain reams of output including statistical analyses. However, every analytic procedure requires certain assumptions be satisfied before the results will be valid. Therefore, users of these computer packages should have a sound knowledge of statistics.

Conclusion

The need for some knowledge of statistics in today's world is obvious. Almost all fields of endeavor are becoming more and more quantitatively oriented. This is certainly true in medicine and health, as a quick glance at the journals relating to these fields will verify. Therefore, a knowledge of statistics is necessary in order to evaluate the results in these journals with regard to their validity. The literature should be read with a critical eye and healthy skepticism. Of course, if you wish to conduct your own studies and report the results, a knowledge of statistics and when to consult a statistician are essential.

BIBLIOGRAPHY

Cochran WG: Sampling Techniques. New York, NY, John Wiley and Sons, Inc, 1963.
Colton T: Statistics in Medicine. Boston, MA, Little, Brown, and Co, 1974.
Daniel WW: Biostatistics: A Foundation for Analysis in the Health Sciences, 2nd ed, New York, NY, John Wiley and Sons, Inc, 1978.
Dyal WW, Eddins, DL, Peavy JV: Descriptive Statistics: Tables, Graphs, and Charts. Publication No 00-1834, Atlanta, GA, Center for Disease Control, undated.
Woolsey TD, Cochran WG et al: On the use of sampling in the field of public health. AJ Public Health 44:16-21, 1954.

6
Health Care Institutions and Levels of Care

Robert F. Gloor, M.D. M.P.H.

History

In 1976, approximately 2.25 million people, or 1% of the population of the U.S., were in health related institutions. About 48% of these people were in nursing care or related homes, 30% in general hospitals and 10% in specialty hospitals (mostly psychiatric). The remainder were in other health related institutions such as homes and schools for the mentally retarded, the physically handicapped including the deaf and blind, alcoholics, drug abusers, the emotionally disturbed, unwed mothers, orphans and dependent children. These residents were located in 34,131 institutions.[1] Not all of these are strictly health institutions, but the vast majority of the residents clearly are institutionalized because of health problems.

All of these institutions may be traced back to the early temples of healing of the ancient civilizations. The prototype of today's hospital is found in the temple of Aesculapius which first existed in the 4th century BC. Physician priests administered treatment and, in time, such temples became the centers for teaching the healing arts. At the time of the Romans, hospitals were developed for the treatment of soldiers and slaves.

It is, however, to another institution that the word "hospital" traces its origin. Early Oriental institutions were developed for weary travelers where food and lodging were provided along with assistance in recuperating from illness. The Latin word for guest was "hospes" and from this root, through the French, are derived the words "hostel" or "hotel", "hospitable" and, finally "hospital". The Christian tradition continued this broad concept and, because of the emphasis on healing brought on by Christian philosophy, began to focus more on the needs of the sick. When Constantine, in AD 335, ordered the closing of the pagan temples, the responsibility for institutions of healing was clearly given to the Christian church. This tradition continued up through the Reformation and, today, church operated and church related hospitals still make a significant contribution to this phase of health care. Parallel to the development of Christian hospitals was the evolvement of a system of hospitals in the Moslem world. This network extended from Spain to western Asia.

During the Renaissance new medical schools were established. The nonprofit voluntary hospital movement began when Henry VIII founded St. Bartholomew's Hospital in England, the first of a network of such hospitals there. Soon, overcrowding forced the hospitals to refuse admission to incurable patients. These patients were then placed in asylums or prisons and the poor conditions in such institutions fostered an image for all hospitals which persisted for some time. Indeed, the concept of the general hospital arose from this experience and led to the development of separate insititutions for the infectious diseases, eg, small pox and venereal disease. Other specialty hospitals came into being because of the physician's desire to group certain patients, such as obstetrical or eye, together.

In the U.S., the development of institutions followed the pattern in England with sponsorship resulting from either a sense of governmental responsibility or the action of voluntary agencies. Other health related institutions have evolved as society has reacted to apparent needs. This evolution continues with the more recent development of intensive care units of various types, the development of outpatient surgical facilities, and growing interest in the hospice concept. Further efforts at decreasing the dependence upon the hospital for all services will progress as payment mechanisms adjust from the traditional stress on payment for inpatient care in preference to payment for nonhospitalized services.

It is impossible to discuss in detail all the various types of institutions mentioned earlier. However, the hospital, playing such a vital role in medical care in the U.S., as well as the nursing care and related home, which will play an expanding role as the number of elderly in our population increases, deserve special attention.

Classification of Hospitals

Hospitals may be classified by ownership simply as follows:

I. Governmental
   A. Federal
   B. State
   C. Local
II. Non-governmental
   A. Voluntary such as under church or non-profit sponsorship
   B. Proprietary

Hospitals are also classified by length of stay as acute (or general) and long term (or chronic disease). The Master Facility Inventory (MFI)[1] of the National Center for Health Statistics classifies hospitals (six beds or more) as general or specialty and distinguishes between federal institutions and others.

The MFI listed 7,271 hospitals with 1,381,267 beds in the U.S. in 1976. These figures represent decreases of 11.1% and 10.9% respectively since 1963 (Table 6.1). The change in the number of hospitals during this period was greatest in the specialty hospitals and, more specifically, in the chronic disease and tuberculosis hospitals with a 70.1% decrease and 91.9% in the latter. Psychiatric hospitals decreased 13.8%. In contrast the general hospitals decreased only 5.2%.

While 5.2% of the total hospitals in the U.S. were federal institutions, they contained 9.2% of the hospital beds. Church operated institutions accounted for 11.3% of the nonfederal hospitals and 15.3% of such beds in 1976; 14.5% of the nonfederal hospitals were proprietary, containing 7.7% of the beds.[1]

TABLE 6.1

Hospitals and Hospital Beds in U.S. for
Selected Years with Change*

	Hospitals	Hospital Beds	Beds per 1,000 population
1976	7,271	1,381,267	6.4
1963	8,183	1,549,952	8.3
change	-11.1%	-10.9%	-22.9%

*Adapted from: Health Resources Statistics, 1976-1977 Edition. Department of Health, Education and Welfare, 1979, p 319.

Accreditation and Governance

Hospitals are accredited by the Joint Commission of Accreditation of Hospitals. Inspections are voluntary and are conducted every two years. Great emphasis is given to records and structure. Recently, the Joint Commission has stressed audit procedures and OSHA requirements. Other reviews are conducted by Medicare, Medicaid and NIOSH as well as by local and state officials. The requirements of the different reviewing organizations may conflict with each other.

The typical hospital is governed by a hospital board, usually made up largely of lay people, who bear ultimate responsibility for the care given in the institution. Governmental institutions have some modification of this type of governance. The board chooses an administrator and appoints the medical staff. The medical staff has its own organization and makes medical decisions, even though the board is still legally responsible. A joint conference committee frequently serves as liasion between the board and the medical staff. The administrator usually serves as secretary to the medical staff.

Utilization of Hospitals

In 1976, there were 36,004,670 discharges from general hospitals in the U.S. for an average daily census of 3.7 per 1,000 population.[1] Even though the number of hospitals and the number of beds has decreased in recent years, the average daily census has increased (Table 6.2). This has been accomplished by a decrease in the average length of stay which in nonfederal short term general and other specialty hospitals was 7.6 days in 1977.[2] The overall occupancy for all hospitals in the U.S. in 1977 was 75.8%

TABLE 6.2

Average Daily Patients, Total Discharges per 1,000
Population for General Hospitals Selected Years*

	Number per 1,000 Population	
	Average daily patients	Discharges
1976	3.7	167.7
1967	3.4	149.8
change	+8.8%	+10.7%

*Adapted from: Health Resources Statistics, 1976-1977 Edition. Department of Health, Education and Welfare, 1979, p 319.

Hospital admission (or discharge) and length of stay are affected by age, sex and income. Both increase with age, and are inversely related to income. Females have higher discharge rates but lower average lengths of stay. While a smaller percent of the non-white population is hospitalized in a year, the average length of stay and consequently the patient days per 1,000 population for this group are longer than for the white group.

Discharge rates vary widely from state to state with high rates for 1967 in the District of Columbia (277.6), North Dakota (223.7), and West Virginia (222.0) and low rates in Hawaii (111.7), Maryland (123.6) and Delaware (134.1).[1] These rates are per 1,000 population.

Hospitals in the U.S. represented an investment in facilities worth $49.7 billion in 1977 with total assets of $72.2 billion. Over three million persons are employed in hospitals. The overall expense for the operation of hospitals in 1977 was $63.6 billion. The expense per inpatient day in nonfederal short term general and other special hospitals in 1977 was $173.25.[2]

Health Manpower

Nursing Homes

In 1976, there were 20,185 nursing care and related homes in the U.S. Of these, 13,312 were nursing care homes.[1] The remainder included personal care homes with or without nursing, and domiciliary care homes. This represents an increase of approximately 21% in nursing care and related homes in the U.S. since 1963 and an increase of 168% in the number of beds. The largest increase has been in those homes providing nursing care. In contrast to hospitals, nursing homes are largely under proprietary management, with 77% of the nursing homes and 69% of their beds being under such management in 1977.[4]

The Medicare Law provided for services, called extended care, for those qualified who needed post-hospital inpatient nursing care. Medicaid subsequently provided for inpatient skilled nursing services for post-hospital patients. Institutions providing both types of care are now called skilled nursing facilities. Another type of care, intermediate care, has been authorized by the Social Security Act for those patients who need health related care in addition to personal care, but who do not meet the requirement for care in a skilled nursing facility. Such care fills the gap between skilled nursing and personal care.

Outpatient Care

Another level of care, home health care, is provided for by Medicare. Agencies providing home health care must provide skilled nursing care and other therapeutic services (eg, physical therapy) to patients in their homes. Such services are provided by health departments and visiting nurse associations as in the past, or by newly developed home health agencies.

In 1976 there were 2,185 home health agencies participating in the Medicare program, an increase of 71% from 1966; 53% were official health agencies, 24% were visiting nurse associations and 12% were hospital based. The remainder included proprietary agencies and those agencies based in other health facilities.

The most widely used level of care is ambulatory care. This is received in the office of the individual practitioner or in the outpatient department of a hospital or other facility. Visits to mental health clinics, public health clinics and similar services are included in ambulatory care.

While total figures of ambulatory visits are difficult to assemble, two major types are estimated through the Health Interview Survey, conduced on a continual basis by the Public Health Service.[5] In 1977, it was estimated that there were 4.9 visits to a physician per person in the U.S., or 1,020,397,000 visits. Females accounted for 58% of these visits, those 65 years of age and over for 14% (6.5 per person) and those under 17 years of age for 24% (4.1 per person). In all age groups, except the under 17 years groups, females experienced more visits than males. In the younger groups, trauma may account for the reversal of this finding.

Again in 1977, it was estimated that there were 1.6 visits per person in the U.S. to dentists. Overall, females accounted for 55% of these visits, and for a majority in each age group, those 65 years of age and over for 8%, and those under 17 years for 27%. The total visits to dentists were estimated to have been 335,202,000.

The last level of care is self-care. Although this term is sometimes used for newer types of inpatient care where the patient performs services formerly performed by facility personnel, self-care[6] includes those actions taken by a person on his or her own behalf in the areas of health maintenance, prevention of disease, self-diagnosis and self-treatment, and active participation in the care rendered by a health professional. The process is complex and varied. A much wider development of heath education resources is needed so that a better informed public may properly use self-care, seeking professional care only, but appropriately, when needed.

Glossary
Pertaining to Health Facilities and Levels of Care

Average length of stay—average stay in days; calculated by dividing the number of patient days by either the number of admissions or the number of discharges.

Average daily census (or Census)—the number of patients receiving care in an institution on an average day; usually the census is taken at midnight and newborns are excluded.

Certificate of need—a requirement that health facility construction, modification or expansion be justified to and approved by a state certificate of need agency. A certificate of need law, approved by the Department of Health, and Human Services, is required under PL 93-641, passed in December 1974. Failure to comply will result in the loss of all federal funds to the state.

Discharges—those leaving a hospital, including deaths but excluding newborns; discharges are usually used in the preparation of reports in preference to admissions because the information on discharges is complete.

Domiciliary care home—in the MFI only those homes not meeting the requirements for personal care or nursing care *but* in which one or two personal care services are provided in addition to the room and board services are classified as domiciliary care homes.

Health Services Area—geographic unit usually having a population of 500,000 to 3,000,000.

Health Systems Agency (HSA)—the agency designated by Health, Education, and Welfare to serve as the health planning agency for a health service area. The overall purposes are:
    1. to improve the health of the residents;
    2. to increase accessibility, acceptability, continuity and quality of the health services;
    3. to restrain increases in the cost of health services; and
    4. to prevent unnecessary duplication of health resources.

Hospital—defined by the MFI as a facility with at least six beds which is licensed by a state as a hospital or which is operated as a hospital by a federal or state agency and is therefore not subject to state or local licensing laws.

1. *General hospital*—a hospital where diagnosis and treatment for a variety of medical and surgical conditions are provided; usually short stay.

2. *Specialty hospital*—a hospital where diagnosis and treatment of patients are provided; may be short stay or long stay.

3. *Short stay hospital*—a hospital in which the average (mean) length of stay is less than 30 days or in which over 50% of the patients stay less than 30 days; may be general or specialty.

4. *Long stay hospital*—one in which the average length of stay is over 30 days; usually specialty hospitals (ie, psychiatric, chronic disease, tuberculosis), psychiatric making up 55% of this group in 1976.

Master Facility Census(MFC)—a system of planned censuses of inpatient health facilities by the National Center for Health Statistics.

Master Facility Inventory(MFI)—a computerized file of inpatient facilities maintained by the National Center for Health Statistics.

Nursing care—defined by the MFI as the provision of one or more of the following services; nasal feeding, catheterization, irrigation, oxygen therapy, full bed baths, enema, hypodermic injection, intravenous injection, temperature-pulse-respiration measurement, application of dressing or bandages, and bowel or bladder retraining.

Nursing care home—defined by MFI as an establishment in which nursing care is the primary and predominant function of the facility. One or more R.N.s or L.P.N.s must be employed and 50% or more of the residents must have received such care in the previous week. There must be three or more beds. Those with less than three beds are not included in the MFC even if nursing care is provided.

Occupancy or occupancy rate—the ratio of the average daily census to beds, usually expressed as a percentage.

Outpatient care—includes that given in a physician's office, in an outpatient clinic, in the emergency room of a hospital, in an ambulatory surgery unit. Outpatient care has one of these three outcomes:

1. transfer to another type of facility;

2. admission to an inpatient type of facility;

3. release to the usual place of residence.

Primary care—the first level of medical care given to patients; traditionally provided by family practitioners, internists, pediatricians, and obstetrician-gynecologists.

Personal care—includes rub and massage, help with bath or shower, help with dressing, help with correspondence or shopping, help with walking or getting about, and help with eating.

Personal care home—an establishment in which the primary function is personal care and in which three or more personal services are provided, or in which medications and treatments are administered in accordance with physician's orders, or supervision is provided over self-administered medications.

1. *Personal care home with nursing*—an establishment in which the primary function is personal care but in which some but less than 50% of the residents received some nursing care in the previous week and there is at least one R.N. or L.P.N. on the staff; or such an establishment without a R.N. or L.P.N. but in which some of the residents received nursing care under other established criteria.

Robert Gloor   63

2. *Personal care home without nursing*—an establishment whose primary function is personal care but in which no residents received nursing care in the preceding week.

Professional Standards Review Organization (PSRO)—created by PL 92-603, providing for professional review of medical care delivered on an inpatient basis.

Secondary care—medical care given by specialists, usually in a regional center.

Tertiary care—medical care given in a highly skilled and equipped medical center such as a university teaching hospital, in which specialists and subspecialists are available.

REFERENCES

1. Health Resources Statistics, 1976-1977 Edition. US DHEW, Public Health Service, 1979, pp 302, 305, 317, 319, 321, 329.
2. American Hospital Association Guide to the Health Care Field. Chicago, IL, American Hospital Association, 1978, pp A-7, A-8.
3. Minority Health Chart Book. Washington, DC, American Public Health Association, 1974, pp 67-70.
4. The National Nursing Home Survey, 1977 Summary for the United States. US DHEW, Public Health Service, 1979, p 8.
5. Current estimates from the Heath Interview Survey, United States, 1977. US DHEW, Public Health Service, 1978, pp 28-30.
6. Levin LS, Katz AH, Holst E: Self-Care—Lay Initiatives in Health. New York, NY Prodist, 1976, pp 10, 11.

BIBLIOGRAPHY

Freidson, E, (ed): The Hospital in Modern Society. New York, NY, The Free Press of Glencoe, 1963.

Guide to the Health Care Field, 1978 Edition. Chicago, IL, American Hospital Association, 1978.

Health Resources Statistics: Health Manpower and Health Facilities, 1976-1977 Edition. US DHEW, National Center for Health Statistics, 1979.

Gaffney JC, Glandon GL (ed): Profile of Medical Practice, 1979. Chicago, IL, AMA, 1979.

Knowles, JH, (ed): Hospitals, Doctors, and the Public Interest. Cambridge, MA, Harvard University Press, 1965.

Misek GI (ed): Socioeconomic Issues of Health, 1979. Chicago, IL, AMA, 1979.

Sloane RM, Sloane BC: A Guide to Health Facilities: Personnel and Management. St Louis, MO, The CV Mosby Co., 1975.

Somers HM, Somers AR: Medicare and the Hospitals. Washington DC, The Brookings Institute, 1967.

Health Manpower

7

Elizabeth R. Ruben, M.D.

The term health manpower refers to the more than five million people in the United States, both professional and technical, who are involved in the delivery of health care and health related services to our population. From physicians to clerical help, they represent a dozen major provider professions, and at least 25 different allied health professions, each with support personnel. In all, there are over 250 different kinds of health related occupations. At least two-thirds of these people are employed in hospitals. In total, 75% are women, though some goups are almost entirely women and others hardly at all. Most of those responsible for major decision making in health care, however, are men.

The major manpower pool is ever changing and expanding. As our population grows, as consumer knowledge and demand for high quality health care increases, and as new medical knowledge and technology continues to unfold, there are new services to be provided, new tasks to be performed, new machines to run and maintain. Perceived shortages in several manpower areas have led to intensified efforts not only to increase their numbers, but also to develop technical support personnel who can be trained in shorter periods of time. Rising costs of health care have led to the passing along of many tasks to new, less highly and expensively trained persons. Each person in these groups has his or her own values and goals, abilities and needs. To assist in a better understanding of who they are and the roles they play in health care delivery is the purpose of this chapter.

Physicians are usually considered the leaders of the "health care team", and the gatekeepers for a large part of our heath care. They make most of the decisions concerning who needs and who gets care and which kinds. They bear ultimate responsibility for the diagnosis and treatment of most disease conditions and they play a major role in determining health care policy.

Most striking has been the change in character of the medical profession during this century. The solo general practitioner of former years often went into rural and sparsely population areas to provide a spectrum of medical,

65

public health and community care. Physicians today are more likely to be highly specialized, to provide care in a limited field only, and to be attracted to the population areas where they can associate with colleagues and utilize the sophisticated technology with which they have been trained to work.

At the turn of the centry, physicians made up one-third and nurses another one-third of all health workers. The remainder were dentists, veterinarians, pharamacists and lens grinders. Today, physicians comprise only about 8% of the total health manpower pool, approximately 425,000 in all, including doctors of medicine (MD) and about 17,000 doctors of osteopathy (DO). The total number of physicians currently appears to be sufficient. Their distribution across the country is very uneven, however, and many rural and inner city areas are not adequately served.

About 80% of physicians work directly in patient care, the remainder being in administration, teaching, research or laboratory medicine. Eighty-five percent of active physicians practice in one or more of the 36 medical specialties or subspecialties recognized by the AMA. Though only 15% are general practitioners, about 40% are probably providing primary or general care. This includes many in the specialties of family medicine, internal medicine, pediatrics and obstetrics-gynecology. Physician distribution across the various specialties is thought not to provide enough primary care, however.

Only 10% of practicing physicians currently are women, though 25% of entering medical students are now women. Members of non-white minority groups make up about 3% of the total, despite the fact that they comprise 15% of our country's population. And although there are currently 126 accredited medical schools in the U.S., one-fifth of our licensed MDs have been trained in foreign schools. In recent years, as many as 44% of newly licensed physicians have been foreign medical graduates (FMGs). FMGs fill about 40% of the salaried house staff positions in our nation's hospitals. Because of such rapidly increasing numbers of physicians in the last decade, poor performance on credentialing examinations by many FMGs, and because they too tended toward specialization in urban areas, Congress has recently enacted rather severe restrictions on their entrance and length of stay in the country.

Osteopathic physicians (DO) are now licensed to practice medicine without restriction in all states. About 60% are providing primary medical care, and the importance of general and family medicine is stressed during their training. This training is now similar in content and in length to that offered in medical schools, though special emphasis is placed on the importance of the integrity of the musculoskeletal system. DOs are accepted into the same postgraduate specialty training programs as are MDs. The distribution of

DOs throughout the U.S. is uneven because there are only nine schools of osteopathic medicine, and full licensure has been granted by all states only in the last decade.

Most physicians belong to that group of practitioners called *allopaths,* who practice the philosophy of medicine (allopathy) that actively attacks the causes of disease by providing a condition (treatment) which is antagonistic to the condition (disease) being treated. *Homeopaths* are another group of medical practioners. They are physicians who follow the philosophy that drugs which produce certain symptoms in a normal person should cure those same symptoms in one who is ill. Homeopathy places particular emphasis on the actions of drugs, and classifies diseases by their symptoms rather than causes. There are about 7,000 physicians who practice homeopathy, either totally or in part.

Chiropractic is a different kind of healing profession. There are about 20,000 practitioners with the Doctor of Chiropractic (DC) degree. They believe that disease is caused by impairment of the normal functions of the nervous system, and they use various mechanical manipulations of the body in treatment. They do not use drugs or surgery. Chiropractors are trained in one of 13 schools, usually for four years, and are licensed to practice their profession in all states. Nearly half of them are concentrated in five states: California has by far the most, then New York, Texas, Missouri and Pennsylvania. There are chiropractic specialties in orthopedics and roentgenology. Approximately 7.5 million people annually receive care from this group of providers.

Doctors of podiatric medicine (DPM) are trained for a period of four years, following two to four years in college, in five schools of podiatry. Podiatrists are licensed in all states, to diagnose and treat, with medicine and surgery, those diseases and conditions which affect the human foot. Podiatry is the smallest of the major health professions with only 7,300 practitioners. Most podiatrists are male, solo practitioners. Some are employed by and perform surgery in hospitals and other institutions. Podiatry has subspecialties in the areas of orthopedics, roentgenology, surgery, dermatology, and medicine.

The profession of dentistry provides health maintenance and the treatment of diseases of the teeth and oral cavity. There are presently 130,000 dentists in the U.S. with either a Doctor of Medical Dentistry (DMD) or a Doctor of Dental Surgery (DDS) degree. The distinction between degrees is one of choice by the school. The training and practice of both are the same. There are 58 dental schools and 90% of graduates practice general dentistry, usually in solo practices. The remaining 10% are in one of eight dental specialties: orthodontics, oral surgery, pedodontics, periodontics, prosthodontics, endodontics, oral pathology and public health dentistry. There are few women and few members of minority groups in dentistry, but this is beginning to change.

The nursing profession is the largest single group of health care providers. Nurses, numbering nearly one million, graduate from one of three types of training programs: a three-year diploma program (hospital based), a two-year associate degree program (usually in a community or junior college), or a baccalaureate program which grants the degree of Bachelor of Science in Nursing. Graduates of all programs are licensed as registered nurses (RN) in all states. Of all nursing graduates, only about 30% practice their profession fulltime, 20% are working parttime, and about 50% do not continue their careers. Seventy percent of practicing nurses are salaried employees in hospitals and other institutions.

Nursing practice traditionally includes several areas of patient care: direct physical care, emotional support, observation, rendering specific treatments ordered by a physician, patient education, disease prevention, and coordination of the many services provided by other members of the health team. Nurses also provide varying amounts of administrative services. Differences in their training and responsibility have led to a distinction between the executive or professional nurse and the technical nurse.

The expansion of knowledge and technology in health care has not left nursing behind. Many specialty areas have been developed, often at the master's degree or doctoral levels, including anesthesia, intensive and emergency care, midwifery, psychiatry, education, and public health. More recently, the nurse practitioner (NP) has emerged as one member of a new category variously referred to as physician extenders, new health practitioners, or health associates. Nurse practitioners provide patient assessment and direct primary care in what is seen by them as a natural expansion of nursing practice. Nurse practitioner training can be obtained in one of several special areas including emergency medicine and mental health. The length of this training varies from a few months to two years and leads to special certification and, in some programs, a master's degree.

Optometrists, with a Doctor of Optometry (OD) degree, are concerned with the assessment and correction of defects of vision. They examine eyes, prescribe and fit glasses and other lenses, and may also prescribe eye exercises called orthoptics. Their training includes recognition of other diseases which may de detected in the eye, and the need for appropriate referral. Doctors of Optometry are licensed in all states, but many states prohibit them from using drugs or eye drops. They do not perform surgery. Most optometrists are self-employed. They number about 20,000 in the U.S.

Opticians prepare and fit glasses and contact lenses from the prescriptions of optometrists or ophthalmologists (physicians specializing in the eye). They neither examine nor treat eyes.

Pharmacists are another large group of health professionals with over 122,000 practitioners. They are trained at or beyond the baccalaureate level in the science of drugs: compounding, manufacture, testing, and their clinical effects on people. Most pharmacists practice in community settings filling prescriptions for medications, and their services are readily accessible to the public. In this capacity, they may be the first to be consulted by a patient when a health problem arises. About 10% work in hospitals, and another small group is employed in the pharmaceutical industry or in academic settings. A clinical pharmacist, often with a Doctor of Pharmacy (Pharm D) degree, may make hospital rounds with a physician, providing valuable knowledge of drug reactions and interactions as an additional facet of patient care.

Psychologists are trained at baccalaureate, master's and doctoral levels to understand and modify human behavior. Some diagnose and treat mental illness in private or institutional practice. Others are engaged in community psychology, research and teaching, or testing and counseling in schools, industries and community agencies. Nearly all states license doctoral-level psychologists. A few also grant licensure to those with a master's degree.

Social workers assist patients and their families in assessing and coping with various elements of the human environment, both social and emotional factors, as they may relate to illness and recovery. Most are employed in institutions, clinics, or various service agencies. Some have private counseling practices. A few states license social workers. Several other states may register or certify them, but do not require licensure for practice.

One more major group requires mention: doctors of veterinary medicine (DVM). That they too are involved in human health is obvious when one considers their training and knowledge in the control of diseases transmitted to humans from animals, eg, rabies and tuberculosis. They guard the health of farm animals—part of our food supply. Veterinary medicine has been involved in the use of animals and animal tissues for medical and surgical research, space medicine and marine research. Their specialties include preventive medicine, public health, and toxicology, among others. Many are employed in the pharmaceutical, biological and food industries. They also supervise the inspection of imported animals and animal products, to prevent the introduction of disease from abroad.

Since the turn of the century, many new kinds of health services have evolved, leading to the development of new types of providers—the allied health personnel. Allied health persons include those trained both at professional and technical levels, and who augment or support and aid the primary providers. Some work directly with or under the supervision of the major providers.

The relatively new group called physician extenders (also called nonphysician health practitioners, mid-level health practitioners, or clinical associates) began in 1965 with the separate development of the nurse practitioner (NP) and the physician's assistant (PA). The early physician's assistants had been medical corpsmen. Behind this development was the idea that nurses and prior corpsmen, with their health care experience, could be further trained in physical assessment and in the performance of many primary care procedures and services, thereby freeing up physicians for more specialized diagnosis and treatment. Both NPs and PAs must work under the supervision of a physician. It was anticipated that this group of practitioners could help particularly to fill a void in rural areas where there is an acute physician shortage. This goal has so far been more successfully reached with nurse practitioners, who are already licensed as nurses, and with whom physicians are accustomed to working. Many states have made changes in their medical practice acts in order to clarify the utilization of physician's assistants. Changes in nurse practice acts have also been necessary. Training for physician's assistants, usually in primary care but a few in various areas of surgery, varies from three months classroom training and 9—12 months in a preceptorship (Medex programs for the medical corpsmen) to two to four years of classroom and preceptor training for the many entering this field now with no previous health care experience. There were an estimated 8,000 nurse practitioners and 4,000 physician's assistants by 1977.

There are three auxiliary groups working with the dentists. Dental hygienists have several preventive dentistry functions including examination and cleaning of teeth, the application of flourides, taking x-rays, and providing dental health education. There are both associate degree and baccalaureate training programs for this group. Dental assistants prepare patients, instruments, and filling materials, and work directly with a dentist during his treatment as an extra pair of hands. Many are trained on the job by the dentist with whom they will work. Others may take special training prior to employment. Dental laboratory technicians are trained in vocational schools or on the job to make dentures, crowns, and orthodontic devices from a dentist's prescription.

Auxiliary workers in the field of nursing include licensed practical nurses (LPN) who have 12 to 18 months of training in nursing skills at a vocational school or junior college. Nurse aides, orderlies, and attendants assist in nursing care after brief on the job training.

Many others in allied health areas have become recognized as highly competent professionals in their own right and have further developed their own support workers. Two of the earliest of these professional groups developed in the area of rehabilitation. Occupational therapists use specifically selected tasks, crafts and exercises in the evaluation and treatment of individuals with physical, mental, and emotional disabilities. Physical therapists make use of various physical agents, exercises and special equipment to accomplish the same purposes. Both of these professions require training at or beyond the baccalaureate level and both train assistants and aides in their respective fields. Physical therapists are licensed by all states. There are several other types of therapists in this area, using recreation, music, education and manual arts to rehabilitate patients. Rehabilitative services of the various types are often coordinated by a physiatrist who is a physician with specialty training in this area.

In the field of nutrition, dieticians and nutritionists are trained at baccalaureate and graduate degree levels in the various areas of human nutrition. Some work in clinical settings to select and counsel on appropriate diets for patients with special health problems. Others work in institutional food service management, in school lunch programs, in community and public health, and in research. Dietetic technicians and assistants with lesser amounts of training work under their supervision.

In the clinical laboratory, under the direction of pathologists (physician specialists in laboratory medicine), are a variety of workers, including medical technologists, medical laboratory technicians and assistants, histologic technicians, cytotechnologists, blood bank technologists and several others.

Other paraprofessionals include respiratory therapists, technologists and technicians in the area of surgery, radiology and radiation therapy, nuclear medicine, emergency medicine, electrocardiography, electroenphalography and perfusion therapy. The newest of these, the emergency medical technician, appeared in the early 1970s. Emergency medicial technicians (EMT) with several grades of training and responsibility, now number nearly 300,000.

There are also professional and support personnel in the areas of administration, medical records, office management, medical library services, data processing, bio-medical engineering, health planning, health education, speech and hearing, environmental services, communication, and medical equipment operation maintenance.

Society has granted many health care providers the recognition and status of "professional". A professional is a member of some service oriented group which claims a unique and special body of knowledge (medicine, dentistry, etc), a code of ethics dictating the application of that knowledge, and the autonomy to regulate itself—including admission to membership, the quality of its schools and curricula, and the discipline of wayward members. The newer groups are struggling for, and achieving, varying degrees of similar recognition with an increase in the number of formal and more standardized educational programs, the relocation of training sites from hospitals to academic settings, and the use of various credentialing procedures to assure quality in their members.

Credentialing is the formal recognition of professional or technical competence. It conveys status. Included are the processes of accreditation (recognition of the competence of an educational institution or specific program), certification (whereby the qualifications of an individual are recognized and certified by a governmental agency or professional association), registration (the listing by an association or agency of all persons who have met their predetermined standards), and licensure (legal recognition of qualifications by an agency of government). Licensure may be compulsory (required to practice) or, in some professions, voluntary (required only to use a specific title). More and more groups are using one form or another of credentialing, not only to assure quality, but to protect their areas of expertise from encroachment by others and to insure their share of public funding for training, research and reimbursement of services.

Changes continue in this large group of people called health manpower and in the smaller divisions within, and several trends can be seen. The changes in educational programs, training sites and credentialing have been mentioned. Other trends include increasing specialization, more and larger group practices, the development of assistants in all major fields, the independent practice of some allied health professionals, and the increasing recognition of the need for continuing education and recertification. The numbers of women and minority group members in the major health professions are increasing. Also, the team approach to patient care by members of differing disciplines is being used in some settings and its appropriateness is becoming more recognized.

Many problems are inherent in such a large and changing group. There are so many separate and extensive areas of health knowledge and care now that no one group can claim complete leadership over the others. The concept of "team", each member giving a special area of experitse to provide coordinated health care, has great merit in theory. In practice, however, many potential team members work independently, sometimes mistrusting or resenting each other, especially new and unfamiliar members. Some struggle to protect their traditional roles in health care, others try to expand what they feel capable of doing. Perhaps as more personnel are trained to work together and to understand each other's areas of expertise, as well as aspirations, the idea of "team" will become a more workable reality.

The shortage of all types of providers in rural and inner city areas persist, and the continuing trend toward specialization leaves the area of primary, coordinated health care less than adequately staffed. Access to the kind and amount of health care needed, when and where it is needed, depends in large on the types of personnel trained and on their distribution.

Other manpower problems should be mentioned. Patient acceptance of new types, particularly those who are functioning in some roles traditionally

Health Manpower

reserved for the physician or dentist, has generally been good. However, acceptance by the physicians and dentists of those whose newly expanded roles may allow them to take over some tasks formerly performed by the doctors has been varied. Some complicated legal problems still remain in the wording of medical and nurse practice areas, and in new regulations formulated to control and contain these new practitioners. Thus, their potential usefulness, particularly in shortage areas, is diminished.

The increasing trend toward formal definition and licensure of several newer disciplines has created problems, especially where areas of permitted practice may overlap. There are currently difficulties with third-party reimbursement for services rendered by allied health practitioners who have gone into independent or semi-independent practice. And the problem of quality control for the thousands of new and still increasing numbers of schools and training programs, the development of standard curricula, and the evaluation of their graduates is an enormous one.

People working in the area of health care have a profound impact on the problems that plague our health care delivery system, not only on the accessibility of care and its quality, but also on its cost. Physician services directly command only 20% of the health care dollar, but their decisions on the utilization of hospitals, laboratory tests, surgery and other services probably affect 75% of total costs. Health care is a huge industry, and a labor-intensive one. New technology here does not replace jobs, it creates new ones. New workers struggle for credibility, better quality in their ocupations and better salaries. Educational costs continue to increase. The new health practitioners and auxiliary workers, created to be more cost effective, are not fully utilized. The costs of illness and disability, including both treatment and social costs, are higher where the personnel needed to provide appropriate, early, or preventive care are unavailable.

Our health manpower is our most valuable resource for the delivery of health care. It is only a part of the whole system, but a vital part. Their appropriate deployment and utilization would go a long way toward solving the problems of health care delivery in this country. And a better understanding of each by the others would make them more truly a team.

BIBLIOGRAPHY

A Discursive Dictionary of Health Care. Prepared by the staff for the use of the Subcommittee on Health and the Environment of the Committee on Interstate and Foreign Commerce, U.S. House of Representatives, February, 1976.

A report to the President and Congress on the Status of Health Professions Personnel in the United States. US DHEW, 1978.

Allen AS (ed): Introduction to Health Professions. 2nd ed, St. Louis, MO, CV Mosby Co., 1976.

Andreoli KC: Ambulatory health care and the nurse practitioner. Ala J Med Sci 14:57-63, 1977.

Elizabeth Ruben

Breslow L: Basic foundations of personal heath care. In Sartwell PE (ed), Maxcy-Rosenau: Preventive Medicine and Public Health, 10th ed. New York, NY, Appleton-Century-Crofts, 1973, pp 649-655.

Credentialing Health Manpower. US DHEW, 1977.

Health Resources Statistics: Health Manpower and Health Facilities, 1976-1977 ed, Hyattesville, MD, US DHEW, 1979.

Kane RL, Olsen DM, Castle, CH: Medex and their physician preceptors. JAMA 236:2509-2512, 1976.

Mauksch IG: The nurse practitioner movement—where does it go from here? Am J Public Health 68:1074-1075, 1978.

McTaggert AC, McTaggert LM: The Health Care Dilemma. 2nd ed, Boston, MA, Holbrook Press Inc., 1976.

Medical Education in the United States 1977-1978. JAMA 240:2809-2910, 1978

Osteopathic licensing summary. Journal AOA Alamanac 77: Supplement, April, 1978.

Reitzes DC, Elkhanialy H: Black students in medical schools. J Med Educ 51:1001-1005, 1976.

Scheffler RM, Weisfeld N, Ruby G et al: A manpower policy for primary health care. N Engl J Med 298:1058-1062, 1978.

State Regulation of Health Manpower. US DHEW, 1977.

Utilization of Selected Medical Practitioners: United States, 1974. Advance Data from Vital and Health Statistics, No 24. Hyattesville, MD, US DHEW, 1978.

Way PO, Jensen LE, Goodman LJ: Foreign medical graduates and the issue of substantial disruption of medical services. N Engl J Med 299:745-751, 1978.

William MK, Weinberg E, Burnett RD et al: The pediatric nurse associate: A model of collaboration between medicine and nursing. N Engl J Med 298:740, 741, 1978.

8

The Cost of Medical Care and Mechanisms for Financing Health Care

F. Douglas Scutchfield, M.D.

In 1975 an estimated $118.5 billion was expended on medical care in the United States. This represents 8.3% of our Gross National Product (GNP). This is an annual per capita expenditure of $547. From 1935 to 1955 there were very small incremental increases in percent of the GNP expended for health. However, since 1965 we have had a rapid acceleration in the percent of GNP expended for medical care.[1]

There are three major sources of these monies: 1) government, 2) the private insurance company and 3) directly from the consumer to the provider as out-of-pocket costs. In the fiscal year 1975, the public or governmental share of the total medical care costs was 42%; 26% of the total was paid by insurance companies, 28% as direct out-of-pocket patient cost, with the balance of 4% being provided by philanthropy and industry.[1] Figure 8.1 examines the allocation of the $118 billion expended for medical care in 1975. This figure illustrates that hospitals were responsible for a major portion of expended funds, 39.4%, whereas physicians, the next largest category, accounted for 18.6% of the total. Table 8.1 shows that the medical care price index for hospital private rooms has risen much more rapidly than either the overall CPI, physician fees or perscription drugs. In fact, the average hospital cost per patient day has risen from $15 in 1950 to an average per deim of $175 for 1976.

What are the factors responsible for the rising cost of medical care? A number of explanations have been proposed. The first is the growth in the number of people with health insurance. As the purchasing power of the American consumer rises, particularly for medical care, in the face of a relatively stable supply of health care services, the cost will concomitantly increase. Medicare and Medicaid are significant contributors to the expanded availability of financing for health care. Supporting this thesis is the substantial cost escalation, particularly in the cost of hospital care, occuring around 1965 when Medicare and Medicaid were instituted.

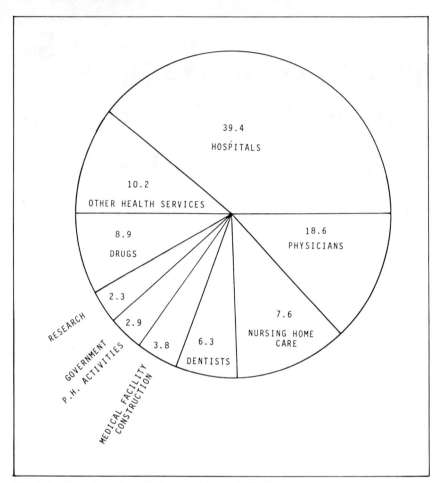

Fig. 8.1. Allocation of medical care dollars, 1975, U.S.

The second possible explanation for the rising cost in medical care is increasing labor costs. In 1974, approximately one half of the total hospital expenses represented employee wages. While this is a substantial portion of hospital's total costs, that figure has dropped since the 1960s.

The third component which is responsible for rising cost of medical care is technology. The current consumer of medical care is purchasing a much improved technological quality of care. For example, in 1960 only 10% of community hospitals had intensive care units; in 1973, 60% of these hospitals had such units. The growth of areas such as computerized axial tomography, coronary bypass surgery, renal dialysis, and other important technological improvements have had a substantial impact on the quality of care. In the medical care sector, however, technical innovations are labor-intensive, not

Cost of Medical Care

TABLE 8.1

Consumer Price Indices with Components, Selected Years, U.S.

Year	Overall CPI	Hospital Room	M.D. Fees	Rx Drugs
1965	89.5	75.9	88.3	102.0
1970	120.6	145.4	121.4	101.2
1975	168.6	236.0	169.4	109.3
1967 = 100				

labor saving. Instead of saving personnel, they actually require increased numbers of specialty trained personnel. Thus, salaries and wages are likely to be substantially higher than the minimun wage, reflecting these personnel's capability of dealing with the new technology for which they are responsible. This is demonstrated by the fact that in 1950 there was an average of two hospital employees for every bed, and in 1973 the figure had risen to more than three per bed.

The fourth point, which is related in part to this technological explosion, is the unneccessary duplication of either hospital beds or new technology. This has occurred primarily as the result of the Hill-Burton program, a federal program which facilitated the construction of not-for-profit acute general hospitals. In 1953, there were 3.3 beds for every 1,000 individuals. The 1976 rate was 5.0 for every 1,000. On any given day in the United States, approximately 25% of the nation's acute beds lie empty. This is particularly true in areas where substantial overbedding exists, such as in southern California where vacancy rates may run as high as 40%. There have been indications that we can "reduce bed capacity by 20% without any harm to health", or "we should close 90,000 beds to achieve a ratio of four beds per 1,000 population in 1981.[2]

Why are these unused beds a factor in driving up hospital costs? It is estimated that it costs approximately $60,000 to construct a new hospital bed; further, it costs almost two-thirds of the same capital construction costs to maintain that same bed or approximately $40,000 per year. Furthermore, at least half, or perhaps as much as three-quarters of the costs of the bed is a fixed cost, continuing whether a patient is in it or not. While some variability exists in staffing ratios so that employees may be decreased as the number of unfilled beds increase, the debt service (funds necessary to pay back the construction costs), equipment, utilities, sales and services and other fixed components of cost continue. Therefore , in order to keep the hospital financially sound, with income equal to the expenditures, the administration of hospitals must

Douglas Scutchfield

amortize those fixed costs to patients occupying filled beds, thereby driving up the costs of the filled beds.

The same thing is true in the case of new technology. For example, if a set level of demand exists for a coronary bypass surgery in a community, a level that would keep one coronary bypass survery team working at its capacity and that community has two coronary bypass teams, then each unit will have only half of its capacity obligated. There is fixed cost inherent in supplying half as many patients with that particular service. This continued fixed cost must be amortized to the patients who use those services, so that, much like the hospital beds, the cost per unit of service must rise when there is duplication of expensive technological procedures or services.

The final contribution to the spiraling cost of medical care is the result of current cost reimbursement formulas used by most insurance carriers. When hospitals or other providers are reimbursed on the basis of their costs, there is little incentive to economize. In other words, if somebody is going to pay the bill, regardless of what it costs, then there is no reason to keep costs down.

What is done to deal with rising costs? Generally, insurance programs have been the consumer's answer to rising medical care costs. Let's first discuss and define the insurance model. If 1,000 people had 100 admissions to a hospital during a year, and each of those admissions had an average length of stay of eight days, this group would have an "experience" of 800 days. If the cost of the bed was $100 per day, this experience multiplied by those $100 would make the total hospital cost of this group $80,000. Based on this experience, each member of this group would then be asked to pay a "premium" of $80 per person per year to cover the cost of hospitalization. This is a "pure premium" because it does not include administrative costs or the cost of insuring. Obviously, in our insurance model we would want people with average attributes. If we insured only the elderly, the poor, or people with pre-existing diseases, they would subsequently use more hospital days, and therefore more money—this is called adverse selection or risk.

There are two mechanisms for establishing a premium. These are "community rating" and "experience rating". Different insurance plans use one of these two mechanisms for establishing a premium. The community rating is just that. The experience of the community is used as the basis for determining the extent to which medical care services will be utilized with the premium based on that community's previous utilization of the health care sector. Experience rating, however, sets the premium based on the experience of a specific group being insured. Experience rating will generally produce a lower insurance premium than will a community rating. In the community rating, one includes the experience of individuals over 65 years of age, poor people, and people who are unable to work because of some pre-existing medical condition. In insuring a group of workers you automatically have excluded the elderly, the poor, and some persons with pre-existing diseases.

There are two major mechanisms involved in the disbursement of funds from health insurance plans—cash-indemnity and service. The steps involved in an indemnity reimbursement are the following: 1) The patient pays a premium to the insurance company. 2) The patient visits a provider. 3) The provider bills the patient. 4) The patient notifies the insurance company that an episode of illness has occurred. 5) The insurance company sends cash benefits to the patient. 6) The patient pays the provider. In this mechanism there is no relationship between the insurance company and the provider.

A variation on the indemnity plan is assignment. In this mechanism the patients, when they visit the provider, assign their right to receive cash benefits from the insurance company to the provider; the provider then receives, from the insurance company, the cash benefits that ordinarily would accrue to the patient. There are advantages and disadvantages to the provider who accepts assignments. An advantage is, the provider does not bill the patient in order to receive payment, because the funds flow directly from the insurance company to the provider. The disadvantage is that the provider, in most cases, agrees to accept whatever the insurance company provides as payment in full for the bill. Therefore, if the insurance company pays only a portion, this leaves the provider with only part of the total bill paid.

The steps in a service reimbursement scheme are the following: 1) The patient pays a premium to the insurance company. 2) The patient visits the provider. 3) The provider bills the insurance company. 4) The insurance company pays the provider.

The major difference in service and indemnity plans is the absense of a relationship between the provider and the insurance company in the indemnity plan.

There are two major types of health insurance: private and public. Private insurance can be separated into three major categories: provider-sponsored, such as Blue Cross by the Hospital Association, Blue Shield by the Medical Association, Delta Dental by the Dental Association; private-for-profit insurance such as Aetna and Metropolitan; and the independent plans or cooperatives such as Kaiser Permanente.

Blue Cross was founded in the early 1930s and represented the first serious attempt at medical care insurance. Blue Cross originated in Texas as the result of an effort by a hospital to assure that school teachers would be able to pay for hospital costs. Blue Cross grew as hospital associations saw the advantage in assuring that individuals had the financial ability to pay for hospital costs. So the hospital association assumed responsibility essentially in each state for the development of the Blue Cross insurance plan. It is important to note that there is no real national Blue Cross policy, but rather a series of state policies which have coordinating mechanisms, such as interstate banks, so that patients with a Blue Cross plan in one state can be treated in other states. The majority of Blue Cross plans are service plans and pay "costs" as opposed to "charges". The hospital develops an audited cost rate for a specific service, such as a hospital day, and this is what the plan subsequently pays for, as opposed to what the hospital actually charges. This is called a "retrospective cost reimbursement plan". There are a number of factors which go into the cost of a specific hospital day, including such things as educational costs and debt service, as well as the actual cost for the direct provision of care.

Blue Shield plans had a later development. Blue Cross pays hospital costs; Blue Shield primarily pays for physician costs. Blue Cross was the original service plan and while most of the Blue Shield plans started out as cash-indemnity plans, most of them are now service plans.

Originally, commercial insurance companies were cautious about entering the health insurance market. During the 1940s, there was a wage freeze as a result of the war. Because of this, the unions negotiated for increased fringe benefits, in lieu of salary. One of these fringe benefits was health insurance. As a result of this impetus, the private insurance companies became involved in health insurance. The commercial plans had a rapid growth during the 1940s, surpassed the Blues in terms of total insurance in force, and have continued this relatively commanding lead in the health insurance market. While the original commercial plans were cash-indemnity policies, increasingly large numbers of the commercial insurance companies are writing service policies.

The independent plans represent, by and large, union sponsored or industry sponsored cooperative plans. Some of these include the Kaiser Permanente Plan, the Health Insurance Plan of Greater New York, and Group Health Association of America. In general, these plans are Health Maintenance Organizations. The independent plan is frequently a combination of provider and insurer, which assumes responsibility for provision of care, as well as paying for it. Payment is usually in a prepaid capitation basis that is characteristic of these organizations.

Coverage by private insurance is extensive but spotty. Approximately 90% of the total population has some type of hospital coverage. Inpatient hospital services are the most frequently covered benefit. Coverage for dental care, drugs and physician office visits is less common.

Group insurance policies return more of their premiums as benefits to policyholders than do individual policies. Insurance carriers point to the cost of sales of individual policies as the factor which drives up the administrative costs. Since group insurance policies are more often experience rated, their premiums are lower than individual policies, which are more often community rated.

In addition to the private plans described above, there are also public insurance mechanisms. The two major insurance mechanisms in the public sector are Title 18, Medicare, and Title 19, Medicaid, of the Social Security Act of 1965. Medicare and Medicaid have been responsible for increasing expenditures by federal and state government for medical care. For example, in 1929 public expenditures provided for 8.9% of the personal health care cost, as opposed to 37.6% in 1974, and up to an estimated 43% in 1977.[3] Given these progressive increases in the expenditures by federal and state governments for personal health care, it is not surprising that there are increasing government regulations regarding the provision of medical care.

Medicare was implemented in 1966 and is comprised of Parts A and B. Part A is called "The Hospital and Basic Coverage", financed by the Social Security Trust fund, with monies generated by a payroll tax on employers and employees. Part B is a voluntary supplemental program that is supported, in part, by general tax revenues and, in part, by contributions through premiums paid by the elderly. Medicare provides benefits for persons 65 and older who are covered by the Social Security System. In addition, it provides benefits to those individuals who are permanently and totaly disabled, regardless of age, and those suffering from chronic renal disease.

In 1972, Congress also made available the benefits of Medicare to individuals who had not participated in the Social Security System, provided they paid a premium to receive both Part A and Part B of Medicare. The Medicare program is usually administered through an intermediary such as an insurance company. The intermediary receives funds for its administration of Medicare policies. The basic benefit structure under Part A of Medicare includes hospitalization, post-hospital home health service, and the use of a skilled nursing facility following hospitalization. Part A is a service plan, Part B is an indemnity plan. The basic benefits in Part B include physician and other professional outpatient services, home health service care and skilled nursing facility care. Both the home health service care and skilled nursing facility care under Part A of Medicare have to follow an episode of hospitalization in an acute general hospital. This is not the case in Part B of Medicare; that is, these benefits, skilled nuring facility and home health services, do not require an immediate prior acute hospital admission. It is important to note that Medicare does not cover the total cost of care for the elderly. It does provide some protection, but a series of co-pay, deductibles and limitations on the amount of benefits available to the patient, make substantial inroads into insurance protection for the elderly sick.

Deductibles include a set amount of money that must be paid by the patient prior to receiving any benefits from an insurance scheme, whereas co-pay is a percent of the total bill which must be paid by the consumer. The limitations of Medicare benefits include cessation of hospital payment benefits after 90 days (if the patient has exhausted his lifetime reserve of 60 additional days), skilled nursing facility care after 100 days and home health care services after 100 visits. Therefore, even with other governmental programs and supplemental private health insurance policies for the elderly, in 1974 out-of-pocket expenses for the elderly amounted to more than $419 dollars per year, a total of 35% of the cost of their medical care.[1]

Medicaid, unlike Medicare, is a joint federal/state shared program. In this program, the state determines the eligibility and benefits and administers the program, usually through an intermediary. The Federal Government, however, contributes a share of the total cost of Medicaid payments based on the relative wealth of the state.

The recipients of Medicaid benefits fall under two broad areas: the categorically needy and the medically needy. All states which choose to participate in the Medicaid program must assume responsibility for the categorically needy. However, the state may opt to cover the medically needy. The categorically needy are those individuals who receive cash payments for their subsistence. This includes individuals receiving old age assistance, the blind, the permanently and totally disabled and those receiving cash payments through the aid to families with dependent children program. The medically needy are those who are eligible under one of the four Public Assistance categories with an income adequate to provide food, clothing and shelter, but inadequate to cover the cost of medical care.

In order to receive federal funds, all programs must have a benefit structure that includes inpatient and outpatient hospital care, X-ray and laboratory services, physician services, skilled nursing facility care, family planning and the Early Periodic Screening Diagnosis and Treatment (EPSDT). The EPSDT, the only preventive program provided for by Medicare payments, was designed to identify and remedy conditions in children eligible for Medicaid benefits. A number of other optional services can be elected for coverage by the state, such as care by podiatrists, chiropractors, home health services, private duty nursing, dental services, physical therapy services, drugs, dentures and eye glasses, tuberculosis or mental health hospital care, transportation and emergency hospital services, and intermediate care facility services. Also, Medicaid will pay the deductible and co-insurance for Part A and Part B of Medicare. It will also pay the Part B premiums for its Old Age Assistance recipients.

A number of new public health insurance plans, or national health insurance plans have been proposed. In one case, additional health insurance benefits have been made available, through the Child Health Assurance Program (CHAP). This coverage is limited to children and pregnant women who are indigent.

The debate about whether or not to insure everyone and the form of such a plan will continue through the 1980s. With any plan, some common elements should be examined. These elements include: benefits, method of financing, whether they are service or indemnity plans, how they are to be administered, and whether they include premiums, deductibles or co-insurance payments.

There is tremendous variation among the states in extent of covered services. In spite of this attempt to provide insurance coverage to the poor, it is estimated that there are still 9 million individuals who fall between the cracks in terms of the provision of medical care to the poor.

Summary

There have been substantial increases in total cost of medical care which have come, in large measure, as the result of rising costs of hospital care. A number of factors have contributed to these rising costs, including an increased number of general hospital beds, the mechanisms of reimbursing, broader coverage of the population by insurance, and the rapid expansion of technology. In order to deal with these rising costs, a number of insurance mechanisms have been developed to assist consumers. These insurance schemes fall into two major areas—public sector and private sector. The private sector includes the Blue Cross/Blue Shield plans, commercial plans, and independent cooperative plans. The two public plans are Medicare and Medicaid, which are intended to assist the old and the poor in paying for their medical care. Health insurance has tremendous variabilities, both in terms of services that are covered under different plans, as well as the percentage of the total bill that is paid. This variability in benefits has resulted in continued out-of-pocket costs for the consumer. Also, the eligibility criteria for some of our insurance programs excluded sizable numbers of the working poor.

The factors described above have resulted in two important trends in American political life: first, an increasing pressure for a medical cost containment policy. The second major policy issue reflects the current press for the development of a national health insurance program.

REFERENCES

1. Mueller G: National health expenditures, fiscal year 1975. Soc Secur Bull 39(2):3-17, 1976.
2. Reed J: Hospital Costs: Biggest piece of the health care bill. Foundation—Baptist Medical Centers 3(2):10-14, 28-30, 1977.
3. Mueller G: National health expenditures, fiscal year 1976. Soc Secur Bull 40(9):18, 1977.

Organizations For Health Care Planning and the Review of Services

9

Robert F. Gloor, M.D., M.P.H.

Background

A number of factors have contributed to the fairly recent emphasis of cooperative planning for health services and public accountability of those services. Among those factors are the recognition that health care is a right, the increasing role of private insurance with the development of medical insurance packages as part of union benefits, and the gradual but steadily expanding role of the government as a payor for services. Increased technology and medical knowledge, the greater number of workers in the health care industry in addition to the physician and the nurse, and the raising of the level of reimbursement for such workers have not only contributed to the rising cost of health care, but have also contributed to the clamor for public accountability.

In Figure 9.1, the potential for conflict between the differing goals and expectations of various groups is illustrated. It is perhaps natural for the physician or other health professional to feel threatened by the concern for accountability. However, the trend toward cooperative planning and accountability is well established and it behooves the professional to understand and to participate in the activities now required by law.

Committee on Cost of Medical Care

In 1927, a group, the Committee on the Cost of Medical Care, was organized as a self-created voluntary agency. Representation came from the private practice of medicine, public health, medical institutions, special interests, the social sciences, and the general public. After five years of study the Committee's recommendations were released. A minority report signed by 8 physicians and one layman was also prepared as were one brief additional

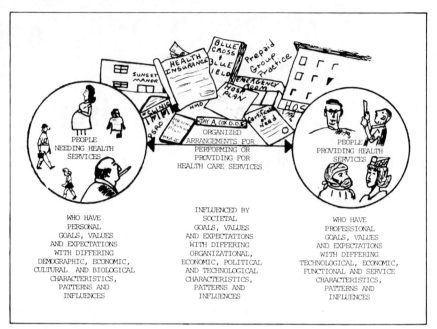

PEOPLE NEEDING HEALTH SERVICES	ORGANIZED ARRANGEMENTS FOR PERFORMING OR PROVIDING FOR HEALTH CARE SERVICES	PEOPLE PROVIDING HEALTH SERVICES
WHO HAVE PERSONAL GOALS, VALUES AND EXPECTATIONS WITH DIFFERING DEMOGRAPHIC, ECONOMIC, CULTURAL AND BIOLOGICAL CHARACTERISTICS, PATTERNS AND INFLUENCES	INFLUENCED BY SOCIETAL GOALS, VALUES AND EXPECTATIONS WITH DIFFERING ORGANIZATIONAL, ECONOMIC, POLITICAL AND TECHNOLOGICAL CHARACTERISTICS, PATTERNS AND INFLUENCES	WHO HAVE PROFESSIONAL GOALS, VALUES AND EXPECTATIONS WITH DIFFERING TECHNOLOGICAL, ECONOMIC, FUNCTIONAL AND SERVICE CHARACTERISTICS, PATTERNS AND INFLUENCES

Fig. 9.1. Health care complex (Adapted from: A Guide to Medical Care Administration Volume 1, "Concepts and Principles". The American Public Health Association, 1969. Courtesy of the publisher.)

minority report and two dissenting statements. It is interesting to review, some 50 years later, the recommendations of the Committee (Figure 9.2).

While calling for group practice, the Committee urged preservation of the physician/patient relationship and the maintenance of high standards of care. The extension of public services for the benefit of all and the removal of political considerations from the appointments of staff for these services was urged. The Committee again called for quality services to "meet accepted standards, such as those of the American Public Health Association". The need, because of the unevenness and unpredictability of medical care costs, for cost sharing by group payment through insurance or taxation, was recognized. The fee-for-service mechanism was to be continued for those who preferred it. Another key recommendation pointed out the need for the coordination of medical services and called for the development of state and local agencies to carry out the functions of "study, evaluation, coordination". The need for the participation of lay persons in such activity was recognized, but the need for health professionals such as physicians and dentists to "furnish dynamic leadership in community planning" was also addressed. The last recommendation dealt with professional education and called for a broadening of the educational experiences of professional students.

Organizations for Health Care Planning

RECOMMENDATIONS OF THE COMMITTEE

I

The Committee recommends that medical service, both preventive and therapeutic, should be furnished largely by organized groups of physicians, dentists, nurses, pharmacists, and other associated personnel. Such groups should be organized, preferably around a hospital, for rendering complete home, office, and hospital care. The form of organization should encourage the maintenance of high standards and the development or preservation of a personal relation between patient and physician.

II

The Committee recommends the extension of all basic public health services—whether provided by governmental or non-governmental agencies—so that they will be available to the entire population according to its needs. Primarily this extension requires increased financial support for official health departments and full-time trained health officers and members of their staffs whose tenure is dependent only upon professional and administrative competence.

III

The Committee recommends that the costs of medical care be placed on a group payment basis, through the use of insurance, through the use of taxation, or through the use of both these methods. This is not meant to preclude the continuation of medical service provided on an individual fee basis for those who prefer the present method. Cash benefits, i. e., compensation for wage-loss due to illness, if and when provided, should be separate and distinct from medical services.

IV

The Committee recommends that the study, evaluation, and coordination of medical service be considered important functions for every state and local community, that agencies be formed to exercise these functions, and that the coordination of rural with urban services receive special attention.

V

The Committee makes the following recommendations in the field of professional education: (A) That the training of physicians give increasing emphasis to the teaching of health and the prevention of disease; that more effective efforts be made to provide trained health officers; that the social aspects of medical practice be given greater attention; that specialties be restricted to those specially qualified; and that postgraduate educational opportunities be increased; (B) that dental students be given a broader educational background; (C) that pharmaceutical education place more stress on the pharmacist's responsibilities and opportunities for public service; (D) that nursing education be thoroughly remoulded to provide well-educated and well-qualified registered nurses; (E) that less thoroughly trained but competent nursing aides and attendants be provided; (F) that adequate training for nurse-midwives be provided; and (G) that opportunities be offered for the systematic training of hospital and clinic administrators.

Fig 9.2. Recommendations of the committee on the costs of medical care (From: Medical Care for the American People, The Final Report of the Committee on the Costs of Medical Care. Chicago, October, 1932. Reprinted by U.S. Department of Health, Education and Welfare, 1970).

Robert Gloor

The principal minority report, while calling for less involvement of the government in the practice of medicine, did urge that the medical profession be relieved of the "burden" of "indigent care" by the expansion of the government's role in such care. The minority joined the majority in its recommendation concerning study, evaluation, and coordination; but felt that such planning and review should be solely in the hands of providers. They also urged greater emphasis on general practice, and opposition to the corporate practice of medicine. While the minority report was signed by less than one third of the physicians on the Committee, it was subsequently adopted by the American Medical Assoication, thus representing organized medicine's opposition to group practice and the community leadership and control of health sevices at that time.

Social Security Act

Due to the effects of the Depression of the thirties, the federal government moved into a greater role in the financing of health services through the Social Security Act. Also funded were the research efforts of the Public Health Service which culminated in the development of the National Institutes of Health. Later amendments to the Social Security Act have greatly increased the involvement of the federal government in the financing area.

Hospital Survey and Construction Act (Hill-Burton Act)

After World War II, the Hill-Burton Act provided for local funds to assist in hospital construction and subsequently, the construction of other health facilities. This funding carried with it the development of structural standards for facilities built with Hill-Burton assistance. Many of the hospitals now operating were financed, through the years, by Hill-Burton funding.

Legislation in the Sixties

In the early 60s, the Community Mental Health Act provided for local community health centers. Again there were developed specific requirements if such centers were to be federally funded.

During this time, efforts to secure any form of national health insurance were unsuccessful until the passage of the Social Security Amendments of 1965 which provided for Medicare and Medicaid. The same congress passed legislation creating the Regional Medical Program (RMP), called the Heart, Cancer, and Stroke Program. The RMP's purpose was to relate the results of research and medical center expertise to the smaller communities by fostering ties for a two-way flow of information and patients, focusing, at first, on the three leading causes of death and morbidity in our country. The original recommendation of the presidential commission which led to the legislation was for the development of centers of expertise to which patients could be sent. However, Congress, under pressure from the AMA provided for ties to improve care at the community level by an outflow of information rather than just by the referral of patients centrally.

Comprehensive Health Planning

With the entrance of the government into the financing of private medical care in a substantial way, it is not surprising that in 1966 Congress passed the Comprehensive Health Planning Act (Partnership for Health Act). This act had as its goal for the nation to promote and assure the highest level of health for every person by:

1) minimizing unnecessary duplication of facilities and services;
2) fostering accountability through improved efficiency and productivity of health services; and
3) developing a more coordinated health care system in order to upgrade the choices made available to the consumer.

State and area-wide agencies were provided for by the act and each was to have an advisory board, with consumers in the majority. Funds also were provided for training in health planning and for funding of demonstration projects. This CHP activity was never funded at an adequate level and some of the area-wide or "B" agencies were funded by other sources. Ultimately the local agencies were to be supported solely by local funds.

Elements of Good Health Care

In 1969, the American Public Health Association addressed the concepts and principles of medical care administration. The elements of good care were identified with their constituent factors.* They are given here not because they were new at that time but because they sum up the basic issues prompting the various groups to be concerned with health planning and accountability. The differences in opinion usually focus on how to affect these elements, not in the basic concepts. These elements and their constituents are:

Accessibility	*Quality*
Personal Accessibility	Professional Competence
Comprehensive Services	Personal Acceptability
Quantitative Adequacy	Qualitative Adequacy

Continuity	*Efficiency*
Person-Centered Care	Equitable Financing
Central Source of Care	Adequate Compensation
Coordinated Services	Efficient Administration

---

*From: A Guide to Medical Care Administration Volume I, "Concepts and Principles", The American Public Health Association, 1969, Courtesy of the pubisher.

Robert Gloor   89

The elements may be defined as follows:

Accessibility—the ability of the person needing health services to obtain these services from the persons providing them.

Continuity—the provision of care meeting the total health needs of the person in a coordinated manner.

Quality—the provision of care which implements the most up-to-date knowledge and techniques available to the health sciences.

Efficiency—the provision of services achieving the desired effect, consistent with the standards of quality, at the least cost.

Professional Standards Review Organizations

Amidst all this other governmental involvement in planning and coordination, the issue of quality control came to the forefront. The concept of audit of the quality of care is not new. The Flexner Report, the development of specialty boards, the movement leading to accreditation of hospitals, the development within hospitals of Death, Tissue and Infection Control committees, all represent efforts to improve the quality of care by the development of standards in various areas. Indeed, licensure itself is designed to assure at least a minimum level of quality by the physician or other health professional or health care institution.

In the early seventies, when efforts toward national health insurance were intensifying, and consumerism was on the rise, amid growing concern that health care costs were getting out of hand, the AMA, among others, actively pushed for the development of peer review procedures. To some, the alternative appeared to be consumer review.

Medicare had required utilization review, but Medicare premiums had doubled between 1966 and 1972. The main concern in Congress at this time was cost control not quality. Thus, in the fall of 1972, Congress passed PL 92-603 containing amendments to the Social Security Act, which provided for "Professional Standards Review".

The purposes of the law are found in Section 1151, "Declaration of Purpose".*

> In order to promote the effective, efficient, and economical delivery of health care services of proper quality for which payment may be made (in whole or in part) under this Act and in recognition of the interests of patients, the public, practitioners, and providers in improved health care services, it is the purpose of this part to assure, through the application of suitable procedures of professional standards review, that the services for which payment may be made under the Social Security Act will conform to appropriate standards for the provision of health care and that payment for such services will be made—

---

*From: Proceedings: Conference on Professional Self-Regulation. *Washington, DC, US Department of Health, Education, and Welfare, 1975, pp 128, 131.*

1) only when, and to the extent, medically necessary as determined in the exercise of reasonable limits of professional discretion; and

2) in the case of services provided by a hospital or other health care facility on an inpatient basis, only when and for such period as such services cannot, consistent with professionally recognized health care standards, effectively be provided on an outpatient basis or more economically in an inpatient health care facility of a different type, as determined in the exercise of reasonable limits of professional discretion.

From this we can ascertain the following purposes:

1) assurance that services paid for under the Social Security Act conform to appropriate professional standards;
2) assurance that such services are medically necessary; and
3) assurance that inpatient services are provided only when and for such a period of time as is required, and only when outpatient care or care in a less expensive facility of a different type is not consistent with professionally recognized health standards.

The wording of the purposes suggest a prime concern for quality control but the sanctions are financial and the impetus for the development of PL 92-603 were largely economic. The conflict between cost control and provision of quality services is not new. The underlying issues are: 1) the role of the consumer in efforts to control cost or quality and the public accountability of those providing health services, and 2) the role of the federal government in efforts to control cost and assure quality.

PSRO legislation was designed to provide public accountability while preserving the confidentiality of medical records and maintaining the concept of peer or professional review of professional activity. The premises upon which the PSRO program was founded are:*

1) Peer pressure is the most effective means of assuring the public of accountability for the health services provided under third-party financing programs;
2) Effective quality assurance requires the establishment of a full-time system of review encompassing all facets of the health care system;
3) Local, community-based organizations are required to operate effective systems of peer review; and
4) Sponsorship of peer review organizations must be external to institutions in order to maintain objectivity.

The mechanism established by law for PSRO is that of professional groups who will establish criteria and norms for their areas by which cases may be audited and by which those cases not meeting the standards are identified.

---

*From Goran MJ et al: The PSRO Hospital Review System. *Medical Care.* (13:4 Supplement 2, 1975). Courtesy of the publisher and author.

Robert Gloor 91

These audits may suggest over *or* under utilization of services, techniques and procedures, since both over and under utilization have implications for both quality and cost. These audit procedures are all to be supervised by professionals and any judgment of professionals is to be by fellow professionals. Review mechanisms of these activities are provided for in the law.

In addition to the activities implied in the purposes stated earlier the Act provides (in Section 1155) for a PSRO to determine, in advance, in case of elective admission to a hospital or other health facility or in the case of any other health care service which is likely to consist of extended or costly treatment, whether such service meets the criteria stated in the purposes of the Act.

The three types of review provided for in the law and regulations are:

  1. concurrent review
     a. admission certification
     b. continued stay review
  2. medical care evaluation studies, and
  3. profile analysis

Concurrent review establishes the necessity of admission and certifies a length of stay according to professionally established criteria, and the necessity for extended stay above that certified on admission. The initial certification both as to necessity and as to length of stay is to be performed within the first working day after admission. Pre-admission certification may be used for elective procedures. Before the expiration of the time period initially certified, the record must be reviewed and if an extended stay is justified this too must be certified at that time. Concurrent review also establishes that the procedures and treatment received for a specific diagnosis meet the criteria for that diagnosis. This is called concurrent quality assurance.

Medical care evaluation (MCE) studies focus on an in-depth assessment of the quality of care in a selected service area or of administrative and organizational support for services. Thus, MCEs are audits of any one of a variety of aspects of care. Hospitals must have one MCE study under way at any one time and complete one study each year. The audit may be of a procedure, a patient outcome, the process involved in patient care, or some other aspect of the provision of care or operation of the institution. Topics for MCE studies may be suggested by the results of concurrent review. While concurrent review looks at the circumstances of the individual patient's admission, care and discharge, MCEs are problem oriented and may lead to revision of the criteria used for concurrent review. MCEs should lead to continuing medical education as problems are identified.

Profile analysis is done retrospectively and patterns of care for individual practitioners, departments or institutions are established. Such profiles serve to assist a hospital in determining where its concurrent review and MCE studies should focus. Profile analysis may point out admission diagnoses consistently meeeting the concurrent criteria and suggest automatic certification, thus allowing the facility to spend more time in auditing problem areas. Such "automatic certification" diagnosis will still be monitored by profile analysis for continued consistent conformance to the criteria. Profile analysis may be used by a PSRO to moniter the audit activities of a delegated hospital, one which has the capability and has been given the primary responsibility for audit of its activities under the overall supervision of the PSRO for the area.

Health Systems Agencies

In 1974, Congress enacted the National Health Planning and Resources Development Act. This, basically, combined the Hill-Burton, CHP, and the Regional Medical Programs.

The planning activities of the CHP agencies were to be continued by Health Systems Agencies (HSA), each serving a health service area. The health service areas were to meet certain requirements:

1) The geographic region must be appropriate for effective planning and development of health services.
2) The population was to be at least 500,000 and no more than 3 million, except in unusual circumstances.
3) Standard Metropolitan Statistical Areas (SMSA) were not to be split, except when these crossed state lines. Then the governors involved had to agree to the split.
4) Already established boundaries for CHP, PSRO and regional planning were not to be split, if possible.
5) Each area was to contain all health resources usually needed by the population and would include one specialized care center.

Again, boards of the agencies were to be broadly representative and have a majority of consumers. The overall purposes of an HSA, as spelled out in the act, are:

1) To improve the health of the residents;
2) To increase the accessibility, acceptability, continuity and quality of health services;
3) To restrain increases in the cost of health services; and
4) To prevent unnecessary duplication of health resources.

HSAs were to be conditionally designated by the Secretary of HEW with full designation coming after the development of a plan. The Act also provided for a State Health Coordinating Council, an advisory body (with representation from each HSA) to the State Health Planning and Development Agency.

The functions of the HSA are similar to those of the CHP agencies. However, new factors in regard to monitoring and implementation were included in the functions of the HSA. In addition, the HSA was to coordinate its activities with all other appropriate agencies, the PSRO being mentioned specifically.

Section 1502 of the act identified priorities in health planning.*

The Congress finds that the following deserve priority consideration in the formulation of national health planning goals and in the development and operation of Federal, State, and area health planning and resources development programs:

1) The provision of primary care services for medically underserved populations, especially those which are located in rural or economically depressed areas.

2) The development of multi-institutional systems for coordination or consolidation of institutional health services (including obstetric, pediatric, emergency medical, intensive and coronary care, and radiation therapy services).

3) The development of medical group practices (especially those whose services are appropriately coordinated or integrated with institutional health services), health maintenance organizations, and other organized systems for the provision of health care.

4) The training and increased utilization of physician assistants, especially nurse clinicians.

5) The development of multi-institutional arrangements for the sharing of support services necessary to all health service institutions.

6) The promotion of activities to achieve needed improvements in the quality of health services, including needs identified by the review activities of Professional Standards Review Organization under part B of Title XI of the Social Security Act.

7) The development by health service institutions of the capacity to provide various levels of care (including intensive care, acute general care, and extended care) on a geographically integrated basis.

8) The promotion of activities for the prevention of disease, including studies of nutritional and environmental factors affecting health and provision of preventive health care services.

9) The adoption of uniform cost accounting, simplified reimbursement, and utilization reporting systems and improved management procedures for health service institutions.

10) The development of effective methods of educating the general public concerning proper personal (including preventive) health care and methods for effective use of available health service.

In early 1980, HSAs began the review of existing services for the appropriateness of those services. There are no sanctions provided for this required "appropriateness" review but open hearings will bring the findings of

---

*From: Public Law 93-641 National Health Planning and Resources Development Act of 1974. Approved January 4, 1975.

the review process to the attention of the public. Any action curtailing inappropriate services must result from public pressure.

Major amendments to the Act in 1979 clarify relationships and responsibilties, provide for increased funding of HSAs, and in general strengthen the capabilities of HSAs to perform the assigned duties.

Certificate of Need

A very significant section of the National Health Planning and Resources Development Act of 1974 was that each state must make provision for controlling the development of health care facilities and services with cost containment in mind. Such legislation is usually referred to as "certificate" or "assurance of need" legislation and provides for loss of license if a provider continues with a program without the required approval. Under the CHP program lack of approval provided only that such capital expenditures would not be reimbursed by Medicaid or Medicare or other federal programs. A capital expenditure is defined as any expenditure: 1) exceeding $100,000, 2) changing the bed capacity of a facility, or 3) initiating, expending, or decreasing the service of the facility.

Exempted from the assurance of need program are the private offices of health professionals as are routine operating and maintenance costs. If a state fails to enact certificate of need legislation acceptable to the Secretary of HEW, all federal monies for health may be withheld from the state.

Conclusion

Public accountability both as to quality and as to cost is now required by law. There appears to be no real difference between health providers and lay people concerning the principles involved. The mechanisms are being developed and the input of all segments of the health care complex must be utilized.

Physicians and other health professionals have much to lose if they are not involved in the dialogues and decision making. They also have much to contribute and a responsibility to be active in the ongoing process as realistic improvements and changes are made in the health care system.

10

Public Health—
A Community
Responsibility

Charles Konigsberg, Jr., M.D., M.P.H.
Hunter G. Taft, M.S.S.E.

The question might be asked, "Why do we need public health—isn't it just concerned with immunizations and septic tanks and isn't it basically obsolite?" The truth is that the practice of public health is needed now more than ever before. With our ever increasing population, improvement in transportation, and a changing environment as a result of new industries and practices, there are more opportunities for the spread of disease.

Perhaps the question isn't so much whether public health is obsolite, but whether it has the flexibility to adjust to changing patterns of health problems and health care delivery systems. Public health departments have some capabilities which give them a particular advantage in the health care system. These are: governmental authority, health data on the community, orientation toward community problem solving, and basic concern with the prevention of disease.[1]

Public health problems are dealt with at every governmental level—federal, state, and local. Development of various new health centers has not relieved government from overall community responsibility for disease prevention, hence health departments are relevant and necessary.

Definition

Definitions of public health vary with the individual's perception of public health. Winslow defined public health as:*

...the science and art of preventing disease, prolonging life, and promoting physical and mental health and efficiency through organized community efforts for the sanitation of the environment, the control of community infections, the education of the individual in the principles of personal hygiene, the

---

Simmons JS (ed): Public Health in the World Today. Harvard University Press, 1949, pp 23-24. Reprinted by permission.

organization of medical and nursing service for the early diagnosis and treatment of disease, and the development of the social machinery which will ensure to every individual in the community a standard of living adequate for the maintenance of health.

McGavran defined public health as the scientific diagnosis and treatment of its patient, the patient being the *community*.

These broad definitions are important only as they relate to the potential of public health. Definitions in health codes of various states vary in their charges to public health. For example, in Alabama, public health is narrowly defined by laws as primarily involved with sanitation, environmental control, and disease investigation, with little mention of medical care activities. Pubic health laws of other states have different definitions. The question of public health flexibility in a changing society may depend on definitions in law.

History of Public Health

Public health is as ancient as mankind. Early civilizations regulated the manner of waste disposal and took other measures which related to health. Various measures were taken in response to epidemics such as leprosy and plague (the "black death").

Early efforts in the United States were in response to outbreaks of communicable diseases and were directed at sanitary reforms. The early history of this country was marked by epidemics of smallpox, typhus, tuberculosis, typhoid fever, and other infectious diseases. Infant mortality was high and life expectancy low. Medical care was largely ineffective in controlling these health problems. There is little doubt that sanitary reforms and improved living standards were the major factors in the control of many communicable diseases. For example, the virtual elimination of typhoid fever resulted from controlling the sources of infection rather than widespread application of immunization. Tuberculosis rates were on the decline well before the development of streptomycin and isoniazid. The development of immunizations against smallpox and major childhood diseases was the first example of direct medical intervention in prevention. Medical care activities, such as maternal and child health clinics, were developed much later.

In response to early epidemics, states and local communities began organizing to deal with the problems on a community basis. Hence, the development in the nineteenth century of state and municipal boards of health and the development, in the twentieth century, of county boards of health. On the federal level, the United States Public Health Service dates back to the earliest years of the nation. The National Board of Health in the latter part of the nineteenth century ended in failure. In more recent years, the continuing efforts of the Public Health Service were incorporated into the giant Department of Health, Education and Welfare, now known as the

Department of Health and Human Services.

Disease patterns have changed markedly since the nineteenth century, when the major causes of death were infectious diseases, particularly tuberculosis, influenza, pneumonia, and enteric diseases. Today, the major killers and cripplers are chronic diseases, especially cardiovascular diseases, and cancer. In addition, accidents (mainly automobile related) have become a major cause of mortality and morbidity.

Basis for Public Health

It is government's legitimate role to protect its citizens. Public health laws are derived from a state's police power and are the basis for public health activities. These laws not only authorize the protection of an individual's health in his community setting, but they establish organizations for enforcement. Enforcement of various parts of public health law may be retained in state health departments or shared with local health departments. Municipal and county governments also may be involved in public health enforcement. State and local agencies derive their powers from the state legislature. These powers may include code enforcement or actual rule making (regulatory) powers. The degree of centralization or decentralization varies, but the state retains preeminence in all cases. The federal government exercises power in public health through its authority to regulate interstate commerce and to tax.[3]

Broad powers are often given to public health agencies. Discretion and application of sound public health principles must be applied in order to avoid appearing to be arbitrary and capricious. Today's climate of individual rights makes it imperative that good judgment be used in enforcing public health laws.

Public health regulations provide a variety of legal remedies. Such remedies to control communicable disease include: compulsory examinations, (eg, tuberculosis and venereal diseases) compulsory immunizations (eg, school entry, and isolation, quarantine, and compulsory hospitalization for communicable diseases such as tuberculosis).

Remedies involved with environmental and sanitation control include: permits, registrations, searches, inspections, embargo and seizures of articles endangering public health, nuisance abatement, civil sanctions, injunctions and criminal prosecution.

Organization of Public Health

Governance

Most public health organizations have a governing body usually referred to as a board of health. Boards of health adopt rules and regulations based on public health law and determine overall policies.

Charles Konigsberg and Hunter Taft

Traditionally, boards of health have largely tended to represent members of the health professions, particularly physicians. Consumer representation usually has been limited. Historically, most state boards of health have had from three to 14 members who, usually, were appointed by the governor. Local boards of heath usually have five to seven members appointed by local governmental bodies or by the governor.[4] In Alabama, the State Medical Association is the State Board of Health, and the public health function of the state is legally an arm of organized medicine; a local board of health is also the board of the local medical society, with the addition of the chairman of the county commission.

Hanlon believes that a board of health should act as the health conscience of the community.[4] Can a board of health legitimately claim to be the conscience of the community when the majority of its members represent health professions or even one particular profession? Boards of health lack consumer input at a time when consumerism in health matters is becoming more of a way of life. A health systems agency, for example, must have a majority of consumers on its board.

Goodenough makes the distinction between what he refers to as the sponsoring public of health departments and the target public.[5] The sponsoring public might be boards of health and governing bodies, but the target public might be lower income people receiving medical care from health departments or special interest groups (subdivision developers, restaurant owners, industry, etc) on the receiving end of public health regulations. With regard to medical care, the use of categorical advisory boards (for family planning, home health, etc) is one approach to providing some target public input. In general, boards of health continue to represent the "establishment". The interests of the public might be better served by a board that represents medical care consumers and civic-minded citizens as well as health professions, avoiding domination by any one special interest.

Organization and Staffing Patterns

All states have a state health agency or department headed by a state health official, usually a physician. While the state health agency may be responsible for some public health functions, it is common to find several agencies or commissions within a state responsible for various public health functions. Fragmentation of responsibilities is common in spite of a trend toward mergers in recent years.

State health agencies promulgate and enforce statewide public health regulations, provide consultation, training, and supervision for local health units and provide direct health care services in some instances.

The development of local units has been most marked in the northeast, southeast and western areas of the United States. The most recent figures show that 1,859 local health units were serving 2,474 of the 3,102 counties of the 50 states.[6] Like state health units, local health units may be charged with some, but not all, public health matters. Local health units are usually the units that deliver direct public health services. Their independence or dependence on state health agencies varies.

Standards for staffing public health units, particularly local units, have been mentioned for years but these are largely irrelevant due to changing funding and programmatic patterns. The size, complexity and qualifications of the staff of a local health unit vary with agency size and involvement in health matters. Many, but not all, still feel that such organizations, where possible, should be headed by a physician trained in public health.[7,8] Local units are often headed by non-medical administrators due to the lack of available or capable physicians.

The practice of public health requires the technical expertise of many health professionals working together as a team. It is essential that physicians, nurses, environmentalists, veterinarians, epidemiologists, laboratory personnel, administrators and the entire health staff consult and work closely with each other for any viable public health program.

In recent years, the reorganization of health agencies at both state and local levels has occurred. At the local level, reorganizations have taken several forms and have been somewhat evolutionary. Initially, the trend was toward city-county mergers and later toward regional configurations. In larger communities, some health departments have merged with public hospitals to form departments of health services. More recently, especially at state levels, we have seen the appearance of mergers of various human service agencies, sometimes referred to as human resources agencies. While excessive fragmentation of health services is undesirable, questions have been raised as to whether reorganizations have improved services.[9]

Public health involvement at the federal level is extensive—beyond the scope of this discussion. The principal organizations involved with public health are the Department of Health and Human Services, the Environmental Protection Agency, and the Occupational Safety and Health Administration.

Financing

Public health agencies receive financial support from a variety of sources. At the state level, agencies receive federal suppport (both block grant and categorical grants) and appropriations from state government. At the local level, financial resources include state appropriations, local governmental appropriations, categorical federal grants, third-party payments and fees.

With traditional direct tax sources of support more limited, progressive health departments are becoming more creative in developing new sources of revenue, especially with fee schedules and third-party payments. Only through these mechanisms will health departments become prepared for national heath insurance.

Public Health Problems and Approaches to Problems

For many years, public health has had lists of services that "should" be provided. Classically, the "basic six" have been vital statistics, sanitation, communicable disease control, laboratory services, maternal and child health and health education.

More recent statements in 1964 by the American Public Health Association added community organization and planning, facilities operation for certain diseases, home nursing care, assistance in promoting and developing resources for the care of the sick, chronic disease control, and research, development and evaluation.[10] The most recent statement (1975) of the American Public Health Association concerning the roles of official local health agencies spells out additional services including mental health services.[11] The statement seems to recognize the changing climate in public health and leaves much more flexibility. It urges local health agencies to attempt to fulfill unmet public health needs in the community. Community involvement is stressed.

Space does not permit dealing with all public health problems and programs. Those problems and programs mentioned are commonly found. Marked variations in scope of programs occur among health departments, particularly between urban and rural.

One feature in personal health care as rendered by health departments is that of outreach and follow-up. Most programs deal with population groups that lack motivation and knowledge. Home visiting and careful follow-up are necessary for patient recruitment and patient compliance. Use of aides indigenous to the area has been of assistance in dealing with specific population groups.

Communicable Disease Control

While it is true that the majority of the dread infectious diseases of the past have been brought under control, communicable diseases remain of concern since none has been eliminated except smallpox.

Public health has traditionally been responsible for the investigation and control of communicable diseases of public health significnce. The Center for Disease Control of the Public Health Service provides epidemiological consultation and assistance to state and local health departments. All states and many local health units maintain specially trained staffs to investigate disease outbreaks. Such personnel have been involved with investigations of Legionnaire's Disease, St. Louis encephalitis, foodborne outbreaks, and many other epidemics.

Venereal diseases, particularly gonorrhea and syphilis, continue to be of concern, with gonorrhea the most prevalent reportable communicable disease. In 1979, 982,724 cases of gonorrhea and 24,558 cases of primary and secondary syphilis were reported in the United States.[12] Almost all health departments are responsible for venereal disease investigation and control. Not only is venereal disease treatment provided, but investigation of cases is carried out. Extensive interviews are carried out for syphilis, and epidemiological treatment of contacts is a hallmark of control.

New case rates of tuberculosis indicate that this disease is by no means near eradication. In 1978, 28,521 new cases of tuberculosis were reported in the United States.[13] Most sanitoriums have closed, and the emphasis now is on early detection and prevention of new cases. Hospital care is short term and usually carried out in general hospitals. Health departments are involved in investigation of cases, outpatient treatments of cases, screening and prophylactic treatment of tuberculin converters and contacts.

Nationally there has been much concern over low levels of protection against immunizable diseases in children. Levels of protection against poliomyelitis, diphtheria, pertussis and tetanus actually declined from 1964 to 1976. Concurrently, increases of the incidence of measles were noted.[14] Sporadic outbreaks of diphtheria and pertussus have occurred as well.

Influenza is a public health problem of major proportion, particularly in the elderly population, resulting in tens of thousands of excess deaths in epidemics and billions of dollars of direct and indirect costs.

Provision of immunizations, including mass programs, is a major activity of health departments. State and local health agencies have figured prominently in the recent swine influenza and childhood immunization initiatives. Health departments are the usual sources of information and assistance regarding immunizations and other health matters related to overseas travel.

Leading Causes of Death and Disability

Most public health problems today are not all likely to be affected by direct interventions as were the communicable diseases. The leading causes of death in the United States today are chronic diseases; heart disease, cancer, cerebrovascular accidents (stroke), and diseases of the arteries. These rank number one, two, three, and five, respectively. Accidents, ranking fourth, particularly automobile related, are leading causes of mortality and morbidity. Any "disease" causing nearly 50,000 deaths a year and over one million casualties would certainly be labeled a severe public health threat. Chronic diseases, such as diabeties mellitus and hypertension, clearly are major health problems and contribute to the toll taken by cardiovascular diseases.

Recognizing the top killers and cripplers as the public health problems they are, public health agencies may be involved in screening programs for hypertension, diabetes, various forms of cancer, and heart disease. Some departments also provide treatment and follow-up for these diseases, usually for the medically indigent.

Maternal and Child Health

Infant mortality continues to be a major cause of death in the United States and particularly in certain states and areas. While infant mortality has declined by more than 50% in the past 30 years, from 33.8 per 1,000 live births in 1946 to 15.2 in 1976,[15] the United States still has a higher infant mortality rate than a number of other nations. Definite variations by race and religion are found in infant mortality rates. The figures are higher for non-whites. The District of Columbia, Mississippi, Alabama, and several other states have rates considerably in excess of national rates. Various factors are involved with infant mortality, including socio-economic conditions and availability of appropriate medical care.

Maternal and child health services are perhaps the most traditional direct personal health services delivered by health departments. For many years, health departments have been major providers of prenatal care and well-child care for certain segments of the population. Some health departments have developed comprehensive maternity and infant care systems which include the necessary linkages for hospital care, high risk care and home follow-up. Public health has become extensively involved with the provision of family planning services through the federally funded Title X grants. Public health departments have become major providers of the Medicaid-funded Early Periodic Screening Diagnosis and Treatment (EPSDT) program, often using nurses to perform the screening. The EPSDT program has been justifiably criticized for lack of comprehensiveness. Federal legislation to attempt to correct this situation is pending. Crippled children services are provided by some health departments in some areas.

Nutritional services are often provided by public health departments with a major involvement in recent years in the Women, Infants and Children food supplement program (WIC). Questions have been raised concerning WIC, including whether it is a true nutritional program or a food distribution program.

Medical Care

Over the years health departments became involved in a wide variety of other direct personal health services. These are usually aimed at specific health problems or groups and therefore are categorical in nature, rather than dealing with an individual or family's total spectrum of health care needs. Public health leadership has tended to shy away from comprehensive medical care programs.

However, some public health leaders believe the lack of availablility or access to medical care (primary care) to be a "public health" problem. Progressive health departments have become more aggressively and extensively involved in the provision of medical care, including the development of primary care centers.

While some public health administrators feel that it is a responsibility of the health department to provide direct medical care, others believe that it should be arranged. One novel approach which has been tried is for the health department to provide some services directly, but "broker" for other services in an effort to utilize existing resources and avoid developing separate health care systems, even though quality may be equal.

Other Personal Health Services

Dental care services may be provided in a variety of ways. While many public health centers provide direct treatment services to eligible individuals, others emphasize preventive care, including education and flouride rinse programs.

Home health services, usually funded by third-party payments, are provided by some public health departments. Health departments face competition from various non-public agencies which are not obligated to provide large amounts of unreimbursed care.

Mental health services through comprehensive community mental health centers are provided by some health departments, although the trend has been toward the creation of separate mental health agencies.

Laboratory Services

Laboratory support is essential to good public health programs. Analytical examinations for personal health services usually include diagnostic bacteriology, mycology, parasitology, virology and serology. In addition, the laboratory may be involved in hematology, pathologic anatomy, clinical chemistry, and preparation of biologicals. Environmental laboratory support should include routine tests on the quality of drinking water and milk products, identification of insects, and a sanitary chemistry capability to support air pollution and industrial hygiene programs.

Health Education

A public health department is often able to provide educational materials and presentations covering a wide variety of health topics. Particular emphasis is now being placed on chronic diseases and teenage pregnancies. Special programs are arranged when disease outbreaks occur.

Vital Statistics

Public health departments are often the official agencies involved with records of birth, death, marriage and divorces. Departments may issue copies of these records for a variety of purposes. With varying degrees of sophistication, state health departments generate data on birth, deaths and disease incidence.

Health Resources

There are a number of functions with which public health may be involved which assist others in planning and providing health care services. Some state health agencies have assumed health planning responisbilities under PL 93-641. Other areas of responsibilities may include health facilities development, health manpower development, health facilities regulation, health manpower regulation and emergency medical services development. In a few states, the state health agency administers the Medicaid program.

Environmental Protection

Environmental health or sanitation is a basic element of public health. It constitutes much more than the mere elimination of filth. It includes all aspects of the environment which might have have some effect upon the physical, mental and social well-being of a individual.

Environmental programs are directed toward protecting and improving the sanitary quality of food, water, air, homes, swimming pools, and the work environment—anything and everything that might have an adverse effect on public health. What is done and how much is done depends on the number, training and experience of personnel working in the field, the availability of supportive resources and equipment, and the rules and regulations of state and local health departments.

People who enforce sanitary rules and regulations of health departments are referred to as sanitarians or by the newer term, environmentalists. Most environmentalists are college graduates with major study in biological or sanitary sciences, supplemented by on-the-job training and special cources. Sanitary engineers also come under the general term "environmentalist" but are graduates of engineering schools with training in the design and operational aspects of water and sewage distribution and treatment plants, air and water pollution control, solid waste management, industrial hyiene and other areas primarily of concern to engineering.

The food sanitation program involves the issuance of permits and regular inspection of establishments where food or drink is prepared and/or served for human consumption. Before an establishment receives a permit, a review of the plan for the facilities and equipment should be made to insure compliance with sanitary requirements. Some states use an alphabetical grading system where A, B, and C based on the numerical scores obtained during an inspection are posted in conspicuous places.

Most states adopt or use the standards recommended by the Food and Drug Administration of the Department of Health and Human Services as the basis of their food sanitation regulations. Environmentalists work closely with managers of food establishments to insure that sanitary deficiencies found during inspections are understood and that prompt corrections are made. Permits are withdrawn from those establishments that fail to meet minimum standards. The ultimate food sanitation program is one in which environmentalists devote more time motivating and training food handlers and less time on routine inspections.

Milk sanitation in one of the important and comprehensive programs conducted by health departments. Because milk crosses county and state lines, the program requires close coordination between federal, state and local environmentalists. Routine inspections are made of dairies, milk tankers, and pasteurization plants. Samples are taken of raw and pasteurized milk and milk products for bacterial examination and presence or absence or constituents pertaining to quality. Dairies and plants are given permits by health departments, and these permits are withdrawn when results of laboratory analysis or inspections fail to meet minimum standards.

Individual sewage disposal systems often present major environmental problems. Local environmentalists advise builders regarding the size, location and design of septic tacks and disposal fields required for each building based on percolation tests, type of soil and expected usage. They also inspect the systems when installed and issue certificates of approval.

In most states, the state health department retains responsibility for approval of the design, operation, maintenance and sanitary surveillance of municipal sewage collection and treatment plants, and municipal water systems because of the limited sanitary engineering expertise available in local health depatments. Local environmentalists work with state personnel in collection of samples and as otherwise requested.

Approval of subdivisions normally is a joint process involving local and state environmentalists. Plans are submitted to the local health agency containing data on the proposed method of sewage disposal and water supply. Local environmentalists review and forward the plans to the state health department with appropriate comments and recommendations. Upon approval of the final plans, work may be initiated on development of the subdivision. Local and/or state environmentalists inspect the systems after installation to insure compliance with the regulations.

Air pollution and radiological health protection programs require specially trained personnel, sophisticated monitoring equipment and laboratory support that are too costly for most local health agencies. Consequently, these programs are provided only at the state level, except in larger health departments. Air sampling stations are established at selected locations based on the number and type of industries and expected pollutants. Radiological health protection surveys are made to protect workers handling radiation producing devices and materials and to prevent unnecessary exposure to the public.

Occupational health and industrial hygiene programs also are usually not conducted by local health agencies because of the personnel, specialized equipment and resources required. Most large industries have their own occupational health and safety personnel. In many states, the Occupational Health and Safey Administration (OSHA) programs are not under the jurisdiction of the health department, but are administered by separate agencies. Local health departments can identify practices which might be injurious to health and safety.

During recent years, solid waste disposal has become a major problem due to the increase in volume and complexity of wastes. Health department personnel permit and inspect waste management operations and attempt to stop waste disposal in unauthorized areas to prevent unsanitary and unsightly conditions.

In the United States, mosquitoes are no longer of major public health importance, except in the case of mosquito-borne encephalitis which occurs periodically. Health department participation in mosquito control programs usually is limited to advising officials on mosquito control and educating the public to eliminate breeding areas around their homes. Mosquito control in most cities is restricted to larviciding and adulticiding operations due to the high costs involved in more permanent control measures such as drainage and ditching.

Rodent control by most health departments is generally limited to giving advice on control measures, primarily proper sanitation. Special control programs are conducted in some urban areas under the federally funded Urban Rat Control Program.

Public and private schools and child day-care centers should be inspected on a routine basis. In addition to inspection of food facilities, the cleanliness of restrooms, availability of drinking fountains, ventilation, availability and cleanliness of clothing lockers, lighting and heating should also be checked.

Hotels and motels should be inspected regularly to determine adequacy of building structure and equipment and overall cleanliness of rooms. Particular attention should be given to the bed linen, ice storage, bathrooms, ventilation, water supply and sewage disposal.

Prior to the beginning of each summer season, organizational camps should be inspected and permitted, to insure that water quality, sewage and garbage disposal, sleeping facilities, toilet facilities, swimming facilities and food service operations are satisfactory.

Health department inspection of housing is usually restricted to cities with many apartment houses due to the shortage of environmentalists and the need to support other programs having higher health priorities. Environmentalists conducting housing inspection programs are concerned with water supply and sewage disposal, vermin control, heating, lighting, ventilation, solid waste disposal, and fire and safety features.

In a few states, health department personnel inspect barber and beauty shops. Normally, these inspections are a responsibility of other boards established for this purpose. Good personal hygiene of barbers and beauticians, and disinfection of barbering instruments between patrons will ordinarily prevent the spread of communicable conditions in these facilities.

Animal bite complaints are usually handled by local health departments working with animal control agencies to determine whether the animal has been immunized, and to insure that the animal is quarantined. Some larger city health departments have animal control personnel on their staffs for this purpose.

Most health departments inspect and permit public swimming and bathing areas. Pools operated by cities and large organizations are usually operated in a sanitary manner. Smaller pools serving motels and apartment buildings require closer supervision. From a health viewpoint, the most important considerations are those which affect the water quality, such as the operation of the filter and maintaining an adequate chlorine residual and optimum pH.

Health departments receive many calls on what may be classified as nuisance complaints, such as what to do with a dead animal, infestation of roaches and rodents, overflowing septic tanks, bad odors, various insects, noxious weeds, bad drainage, junked cars, animals getting into garbage, etc. All complaints should be investigated to determine if a health hazard exists and that proper measures are taken to obtain abatement. If a health hazard cannot be identified, the complaint should be referred to the authority having jurisdiction.

The U.S. Food and Drug Administration of the Department of Health and Human Services supervises the sanitary quality of shellfish shipped in interstate commerce. Each shellfish shipping state adopts laws and regulations for sanitary control of shellfish, makes sanitary and bacteriological surveys of growing areas, inspects shellfish processing plants and conducts other inspections, laboratory investigations and control measures as necessary. The states issue certificates to qualified shellfish shippers and forward copies to the Food and Drug Administration. The FDA reviews each state's control program and either endorses or withholds endorsement of its program. A list of all approved interstate shellfish shippers is published semi-monthly by the FDA and is distributed to all health and interested governmental agencies. Most health departments take representative samples of processed shellfish for laboratory analysis to insure that the product meets sanitary standards at the point of sale to the public.

All health departments should have contingency plans on the actions to take following major emergencies and distasters, such as tornados, windstorms, floods, major fires and explosions. Health departments have personnel to help manage the injured and sick persons and recommend environmental precautions that should be taken. Food supplies may have to be inspected and condemned. Emergency shelters for dislocated persons should be checked to prevent overcrowding and to insure that all food and water served is safe for consumption. Advice on disinfection of municipal and individual water supplies, control of insects and rodents and disposal of human waste and garbage may have to be given. Having a basic plan will lessen the time required for the health department to respond and will help insure that major sanitary precautions are considered.

Public Health—Interactions with the Community—Conclusions

Public health has had to interface with physicians and organized medicine since its inception. Clearly, this interface has had some significant effects on the development of personal health services over the years, perhaps in a tendency for public health to limit its domain to more traditional areas. While such limitations imposed on public health medical care activities may still be prevalent in some rural areas, they are more of a historical than active influence.

Voluntary agencies have played major roles in public health. For example, the Tuberculosis Association (now Lung Association) was a great influence in the progress made in controlling tuberculosis. Public health and voluntary agencies have often worked together in partnerships.

The proliferation of federally funded direct health care programs has had a profound effect on public health. Federal programs are often categorical (eg, family planning, EPSDT, WIC), a condition which makes efficient and comprehensive provision of services difficult. Special interest groups continue to perpetuate this state of affairs. Non-categorical funding for basic public health services has become increasingly difficult to obtain at all levels of government.

Federal government funding shapes policies in another manner: much money has gone into the development of so-called comprehensive community health centers, which usually do not have governmental sanction to protect the public's health. It would appear that public health has been losing out in the competition for such funds either because of its own reluctance to get involved in comprehensive care or because the funds have been steered away to non-profit corporations. In any case, federal funding seems to have fostered more fragmentation, duplication and overlap.

A successful public health program must compete in the political arena. Public health leadership over the years has tended to shy away from involvement in politics. Political involvement does not mean campaigning for candidates, which is inappropriate for public employees, but does mean making personal contacts with elected officials, being in a position to influence trends and directions of planning agencies, and becoming visible and involved in communities.

Much has been said and written about the "image" of public health and the presumed obsolescence of public health in our modern society. The future of public health will depend largely on dynamic leadership which has the courage to get involved in non-traditional activities, particularly medical care, while continuing appropriate health protection and environmental control activities.

REFERENCES

1. Terris M: The role of the public health department. Bull NY Acad Med, 41: 60-62, 1965.
2. McGavran EG: Scientific diagnosis and treatment of the community as a patient. JAMA 162:724, 1956.
3. Grad FP: Public Health Law Manual, Washington DC, American Public Health Association, , 1970, pp 1-26.
4. Hanlon JJ: Public Health Administration and Practice. St Louis, MO, The CV Mosby Co, 1974, pp 187, 189.
5. Goodenough WH: Agency structure as a major source of human problems in the conduct of public health programs. A J Public Health 55:1068, 1965.
6. Directory of Local Health and Mental Health Units. US DHEW, Public Health Service, 1969, p 115.
7. Jekel JF et al: The impact of non-physician health directors on full-time public health coverage in Connecticut. A J Public Health 70:73-74, 1980.
8. Atwater JB: Must local health officers be physicians? A J Public Health 70:11, 1980.
9. Shonick W et al: Reorganization of health agencies by local governments in American urban centers: what do they portend for "public health?" Milbank Mem Fund Q, 55:237-238, 1977.
10. Policy statement, the local health departments' services and responsibilities. A J Public Health 54:131-139, 1964.
11. The role of official local health agencies. A J Public Health 65:189-193, 1975.
12. Morbidity and Mortality Weekly Report, US DHEW, Public Health Service, Center for Disease Control, 28 (51):611, 1980.
13. Morbidity and Mortality Weekly Report, Annual Summary 1978. US DHEW, Public Health Service, Center for Disease Control, 1979, p 13.
14. Hinman AR: Immunization initiative—a cooperative effort to prevent a national health crisis. Public Health Currents (Ross Laboratories) 17(5):23-26, 1977.
15. Infant mortality in the United States. Statistical Bulletin, Metropolitan Life Insurance Co, 59(3): 2-4, 1978.

Occupational Health 11

Terence R. Collins, M.D., M.P.H.

Currently there is great interest in the environment. Both the work that is done and the surroundings in which it is done have become major areas of social concern. These issues are critical to the consideration of the porblems involved in occupational health and safety. It is the purpose of this discussion to bring into focus those issues which are most important in the field of occupational health and safety by broadly reviewing the history and the present scope of the problems involved. By examining the areas of difficulty in dealing with these problems and reviewing the specifics of ocupational history, an approach to a full evaluation of an occupational health problem will be developed.

Interest in occupational health is not new, as is seen from the following quotation from Bernardino Ramazzini, often called the Father of occupational medicine. He wrote in 1713:

> There are many things that a doctor on his first visit to a patient ought to find out. I may venture to ask one more question: What occupation does he follow? Though this question may be concerned with the exciting causes, yet I regard it as well timed or rather indispensable, and it should be particularly kept in mind when the patient to be treated belongs to the commmon people. In medical practice, however, I find that attention is hardly ever paid to this matter, or if the doctor in attendance knows it without asking, he gives little heed to it, though for effective treatment, evidence of this sort has the utmost weight.*

The major focus of occupational medicine has been the on-the-job injury. For many years the worker had no opportunity to obtain compensation for work-related injuries except by suing his employer. When this happened the worker had to prove employer negligence in order to be compensated. Because of this burden, the mechanism of court-awarded workmen's compensation was never very effective.

---

*From Ramazzini B: Diseases of Workers, De Morbis Artificum. *Translated by Wright WC, New York NY, Hafner Publishing Company, 1969, p 13. Used by permission of the New York Academy of Medicine Library.*

As can be seen in the chronological summary below, the development of interest in workers' health has been slow and tedious.

1700: B. Ramazzini, the Father of occupational medicine, was the first to point out the importance of work in the total health of an individual.
1775: Sir Percival Pott links carcinoma of the scrotum to chimney sweeps.
1833: The English Factory Acts showed interest in worker safety.
1842: Child Labor Laws in Massachusetts were the first efforts to protect a specific working group.
1910: The first Workmen's Compensation laws were enacted in Germany and recognized workers' rights.
1910: The first U.S. Workmen's Compensation law was passed in New York, for the first time protecting the American worker.
1936: The Public Contracts Act established labor standards on government contracts, including those for health and safety.
1948: All states in the U.S. were covered by Workman's Compensation Insurance.
1970: The Occupational Health Safety Act established minimum standards for health and safety of most American workers.

From the onset of the first workmen's compensation laws in 1910, there has been a continual struggle between regulatory agencies and the industrial community as to the type of evaluation and the amount of compensation that workmen should receive for injuries or disabilities incurred in the course of their labor. The Occupational Health and Safety Act of 1970 was the first real effort on a national scale to impose significant standards in order to protect the health of workers. The Occupational Safety and Health Administration (OSHA), the agency responsible for the policing of this act, is housed in the Department of Labor, while the medical expertise is obtained from the National Institute of Occupational Safety and Health (NIOSH), in the Department of Health and Human Services. However, NIOSH has no enforcement powers. This separation of medical expertise and police powers has resulted in long delays in implementation of necessary health and safety standards in industry.

The magnitude of the problem of occupational health and safety is not well understood by the public nor the medical profession. In 1977, at least 13,000 people were killed on the job, nine million were accidentally injured, and 2.3 million were temporarily or permanently disabled.[1] It is estimated that there are 500,000 new cases of occupational disease each year.[2] But these figures are deceiving, since mandatory reporting of occupational illness is extremely poor. For example, a recent University of Washington study documented that out of a group of 600 workers in six different production plants, over one-third of the workers' illnesses were job related. For that same group of workers, the Washington State Worker's Compensation statistics reflected only 3% of the occupational diseases reported by this study.[3]

The area of occupational carcinogenesis is an extremely difficult problem because of the long incubation period and the complexity of chemical exposures and potential chemical interactions in the workplace. It is estimated that many cancers now being treated resulted from occupational exposure, one of the best known examples being the association of asbestos exposure with lung cancer and peritoneal mesothelioma. It has been noted in studies of heavily exposed workers that approximately 20% to 25% of deaths among asbestos workers 20 or more years from onset of exposure are found to be from lung cancer, seven to ten percent from mesothelioma, and four percent from cancer of other sites. Cigarette smoking significantly increases the lung cancer risk of asbestos exposure and aggravates asbestosis, a form of pneumoconiosis.[4]

One of the reasons the occupational health field has been slow in developing is the lack of trained physician specialists in this field. The specialist in occupational medicine is certified by the American Board of Preventive Medicine in Occupational Medicine. The required training is three years residency, one of which is an academic year consisting of a Master of Public Health or equivalent degree. The remainder of the time is spent in clinical training in fields such as ear, nose, and throat, opthalmology and emergency medicine, with varying amounts of experience in toxicology and onsite industrial medicine. Many board certified specialists in the field of occupational health have not had such training and have received certification on the basis of past experience. Residency training in this field has been lagging since the early 1960s, but currently is receiving increased impetus from an infusion of funds from the federal government to support training.

Who, then, delivers services in the field of occupational health? Estimates of workers who receive no occupational health services range as high as 80%. In 1970, 43% of the work force worked in locations where there were less than 250 employees; 26% in workplaces of 250—1,000, and 31% of the work force areas where there were over 1,000 employees. This illustrates the fact that only a very large business could support a full-time physician in the field of occupational medicine. Those companies which do supply some occupational health services do so either by the presence of a registered nurse, or by having a consultant or contract physician who performs their physical examinations and responds to emergencies that arise. There is some effort by occupational health practitioners to set up independent practices and to contract to individual companies rather than be employeed full-time by one specific company. This trend would support more services to a larger number of workers, and in addition would relieve the physician of some of the ethical problems which a company-employed physician must of necessity face when health and safety decisions must be made which might be contrary to company policy or which might impose significant financial burdens on the company. Some unions have employed full-time physicians, but the majority of unions use consultant physicians for advice; the number of such physicians is probably well below the required level necessary to provide adequate health input for negotiations and ongoing consultation. With the preceding information as background it would seem that the role a practicing physician must assume in occupational health is, and will continue to be, a major one.

One of the first decisions that a physician must confront is, what is a work-related illness? To be considered occupational, a disease must be compatible with the effects of a disease producing agent or agents and exposure must be documented. Secondly there should be sufficient exposure, either past or present, to account for this disease, and third, there must be evidence to suggest that etiologic components of this disease relate to the occupational setting. Unfortunately, there is no clear cut guideline to say that a particular condition is work-related. Thus, it is the physician who must make a decision, often on evidence which might be considered insufficient. There are likely to be differences of opinion and these frequently lead to legal actions which eventually decide the case.

In the case of injury, the link between occupation and pathology is relatively clear. There is a problem, however, when the case of ocupational injury deals with aggravation of a previously existing condition. There is no method in the present system of workmen's compensation by which aggravation of pre-existing disease or physical impairment may be clearly defined. It is generally accepted that if an existing disease can be documented, occupational exposure can make this disease compensable if reactivation can be demonstrated. Examples would be a patient with liver disease aggravated by exposure to chemicals, or an employee with known allergies who is exposed to either chemicals or allergens which aggravate the allergies leading to subsequent asthma attacks.

The existence of conditions before exposure does not necessarily mean before employment. Many industries change products, chemicals, and procedures as time passes so that exposure may occur after an individual has worked at a plant for many years. The interests of employee and employer are best served if the private physician is totally objective and frank in making a determination of occupational aggravation of a condition.

One of the major areas of current interest in dealing with aggravation of disease is that of stress. Stress has been demonstrated to be a compensable aggravating factor in such jobs as fire fighting, police work, and air traffic control. Current research suggests that women in the work force may be subject to special stress because of the type of jobs in which they are employed and the additional burden of family obligations. Women tend to be segregated into a narrow range of occupations: 34% in clerical work, 22% in the service sector, 15% in factory work, mostly textiles, and only 8% in skilled crafts or management.[5]

The problem of chronic disease is complicated by the fact that the progress of the disease may be irregular, thus demonstration of occupational effects on the disease will be difficult to document. Time of life of onset of symptoms often will be crutial to this determination.

Most decisions regarding occupationally related illness involve the Workmen's Compensation insurance system. One of the purposes of instituting a system for reimbursement of injured workers was to increase the safety precautions that existed in the workplace. In looking at safety statistics as compiled from the 1920s to the 1970s, the risk of serious work accidents has been appreciably reduced, but there is an important question whether research findings are favorable to the argument that reductions in work injuries had a significant relationship to improvements in workmen's compensation. A supporting argument is that motor vehicle fatalities in the workplace failed to show a similar downward trend. Similar trends in accidents have applied to the home and public fatal accidents, rendering correlation between workplace accidents and workmen's compensation difficult to justify. The workmen's compensation system has filled a void in health insurance coverage, but there are still several defects which affect the worker. In the past, many health insurance policies would not pay when there was a possibility that it might be a workmen's compensation case. In addition, the actual dollars paid to an individual on workmen's compensation are lower than commonly believed. Hence the belief that malingering is a source of inflation of workmen's compensation costs probably cannot be well documented because the process of malingering usually does not result in significant gain. In many cases, if the disability proves to be serious and lengthy, the situation results in court settlement for final determination of compensation.

The confidentiality of a worker's records presents special problems. An explicit policy of confidentiality should be developed between workers and management. This policy should spell out what specific health information should be made available to the employer. The responsibility rests with the physician to protect other medical information which may be in the record.

The physician, then, must be in a position to evaluate the worker. As part of the evaluation of an occupationally related injury or illness, a determination of disability must be made. Yet, little or no time is devoted to disability evaluation in the medical education system, for either medical students or residents. More than an anatomic description of the disability, eg, extension of the elbow limited to 150°, is required. A functional assessment must be made, based on the physician's total knowledge of the patient and the work environment. This disability assessment requires a commitment of time on the part of the physician and is an integral part of the delivery of comprehensive medical care.

One of the common roles of medicine is the performance of pre-employment physical examinations. Pre-employment examinations are common in many industries. In many cases, the forms are designed by individuals who are unfamiliar with the epidemiology of accidents or chronic diseases and the correct questions are not asked, though guidelines are available.[6] It is the responsibility of the physician to assist companies in developing adequate pre-employment physical examination protocols. Some heavy industries require pre-employment back x-rays. If an individual has any abormality, whether it is known to be related to the development of symptoms or not, the worker will be disqualified for hiring because of the company's experience that back complaints coupled with abnormal x-ray findings have led to large compensation settlements. Arguments against pre-employment exams can be leveled, just as for physical exams, that the return is not worth the cost, but this debate is beyond the scope of the present discussion.

The most significant part of an occupational examination is the occupational history. Figure 11.1 outlines the basic occupational history. In many cases, much of the information should be part of a complete history, as already taken by the health professional. There are special portions of the occupational history which must be asked if the physician is to have a high index of suspicion regarding occupational etiology. Stress must be qualitatively evaluated and, if possible, some attempt should be made to determine how much of life stress is related to the job and how much to the home. As difficult as this may be, this evaluation is absolutely necessary if one is to make a determination of a compensable condition. Intercurrent illness and exacerbation of illness of non-occupational etiology must be included. Examples of these would be chronic bronchitis secondary to exposure to irritant gases, fumes and dusts, and varicose veins secondary to extended standing on hard surfaces. Smoking history should be obtained routinely, especially if the condition is related to the respiratory or cardiovascular systems. Inquires should be made about previous occupational disease. The individual may not initially give the correct answer to this question as research suggests that workers with job related injuries seem to be more susceptible to having other work-related problems, thus being reluctant to admit past occupational disorders.

The specific occupational history involves actual inquiry into the job title, which is not of great help because the titles given to workers do not actually reflect what work they perform. The physician must ask specifically what task is done and ask for a demonstration of the exact body position in which the work is performed. Whether this be kneeling, as in the case of a farm worker, or a repetitive motion of the arm, forearm, or shoulder at a particular machine in a factory setting may be critical in the assessment of the etiology of the problem. Inquiry must be made as to the use of safety precautions and

CLINICAL HISTORY

A. STRESS
B. INTERCURRENT ILLNESS
C. EXACERBATION OF NON-OCCUPATIONAL ILLNESS
D. PREVIOUS OCCUPATIONAL DISEASE
E. SMOKING HISTORY

OCCUPATIONAL HISTORY

A. JOB TITLE

   1. Job description
   2. Location and position of work
   3. Safety precautions required and used

B. EXPOSURE

   1. Toxicology
   2. Threshold Limit Value
   3. Maximum Allowable Concentration
   4. Duration and intensity
   5. Evaluation
   6. Multiple exposure
   7. Cumulative - life work history

C. INDEX OF SUSPICION

   1. Other workers with similar illness
   2. Diseases with potential occupational etiology

D. MEDICAL LEGAL RESPONSIBILITY

Fig. 11.1. The occupational history.

whether they are readily available and comfortable. In many cases safety devices are prescribed, but are exceedingly uncomfortable and employees routinely ignore their use. Documentation is essential in either case.

Terence Collins 119

In the course of taking an occupational history, some assessment of exposure must be attempted. It is estimated that over 12,000 chemicals are being used in American industry. It is obvious that all health professionals cannot be toxicologists, but it is important that if a physician is involved with a specific company he familiarize himself with the exposures and the toxicology of the major chemicals involved in that particular industry. In the process of researching these issues, the terms TLV and MAC will appear in the literature. *Threshold limit value (TLV)* reflects a time weighted average exposure, which is empirically determined and has been used as a guideline for evaluation. *Maximum allowable concentration (MAC)*, is a guideline to assist in the evaluation of exposure.

If possible, it is important to know the duration and intensity of the exposure. Unfortunately, many workers do not know what chemicals they are exposed to, and when inquiry is made they may not be given the correct information by management. The average exposure is usually of no help. In most environmental exposures there are widely varying concentrations and it is important to know the peak concentrations and the duration. This must be determined if a dose response relationship is to be considered. In addition, toxic effects differ in onset and severity by route of absorption. There may be multiple exposures which might be additive, neutralizing, synergistic, or potentiating in biological effects. On occasion it might be necessary to obtain a cumulative history of the worker's exposure. This presents extreme difficulties in recall and limits the quality of data collection, but in certain cases will be highly rewarding.

The question must arise: how will a practicing health professional be able to evaluate these issues? This is extremely difficult and, when indicated, professional consultation is required. An industrial hygienist is trained in the measurement sciences and toxicology, and possesses the specific types of equipment which measure and evaluate environmental exposures and can assist in the development of the information needed for such evaluation.

The key issue in occupational health is the development of a high index of suspicion on the part of the history taker. The question which must be asked is: Do other workers have a similar illness? This will open up an entire spectrum of epidemiology which would not otherwise be apparent to the person doing the evaluation. In developing this index of suspicion the health professional must be aware of diseases with potential occupational etiology such as aplastic anemia, hepatitis, nephrosis, epithelioma of the bladder or recurrent bronchitis. Figure 11.2 lists some common diseases with their etiologies which must be considered in this regard.

The physician also has certain legal responsibilities to the patient. Despite the fact that many physicians are reluctant to be involved in situations where courtroom action might develop, it is essential that the medical profession be

1. Peripheral neuropathy - mechanical and trauma effects, chemical exposures, e.g., insecticides, arsenic.

2. Asthma and pulmonary diseases - numerous chemicals, dust, e.g., cotton (farmer's lung), bagasse (hemp), allergic alveolitis.

3. Insecticide poisoning - especially at risk where air spraying is concentrated.

4. Parkinsonism - chemicals such as carbon disulfide and manganese.

5. Behavior disorders - often overlooked, but can be caused by carbon monoxide, carbon disulfide, lead, mercury, methylchloride, and many other chemicals.

6. Hearing loss - this relates to individual susceptibility but it is highly related to exposure to industrial noise.

7. Musculoskeletal disease - arthritis secondary to chronic trauma, especially of the elbows and shoulders; back problems, tendonitis.

Fig 11.2. Some potential occupationally related problems

involved in making these determinations. Non-involvement results in detrimental effects on the patient in two ways: the patient is deprived of legal rights under the workmen's compensation laws and subsequent compensation for injury or disability; and, the worker's health may be jeopardized because he is left in a setting of continued exposure to a harmful environment.

The role of the health professional, in addition to the evaluation of the individual worker, is that of an active participant in preventive medicine. Since all occupational problems are man made, all should be preventable. How can the physicians involve themselves in this kind of activity? Accident prevention should be actively pursued as part of the plan whenever individuals are seen regarding work environments or should be actively discussed at the time of the pre-employment physical. These physicals should function as a vehicle for proper job placement to best utilize the skills of the worker in the context of any health limitations. The exam should also serve to protect the worker from potential harmful exposures. There should be periodic exams for early detection of occupationally related problems. Appropriate laboratory tests should be available and ordered by the physician to detect abnormalities.

Finally, the physician has a responsibility to assume an activist role in encouraging groups to be interested in health in the workplace. Workers should be involved in programs to improve the wearing of protective devices. Programs should also be developed in the community to encourage health and safety before a plant is built. The physician must be willing to take the leadership in developing and participating in educational programs for both labor and management. Occupational medicine is not solely a specialty unto itself: it is part of the practice of many physicians across many specialty lines. Only when physicians become cognizant of the health problems of the patient as they relate to the workplace can the terrible cost in lives and suffering be reduced.

REFERENCES

1. Accident Facts. Chicago, IL, National Safety Council, 1978, pp 23-27.
2. Finn P: Occupational safety and health education in the public schools. Prev Med 7:245, 1978.
3. Occupational Illness. Workmen's compensation doesn't work. Consumer Commission of the Accreditation of Health Services Quarterly, Fall, 1977.
4. Richmond J: Physician advisory on asbestos. US DHEW, Public Health Service, April 25, 1978.
5. Stellman J: Occupational hazards of women: an overview. Prev Med 7:282, 1978.
6. Guiding Principles of Medical Examinations in Industry. Chicago, IL, AMA, 1973.

BIBLIOGRAPHY

Coe, J: The physician's role in sickness absence certification: a reconsideration. J Occupatl Med 17:722, 1975.

Disability evaluation under social security: a handbook for physicians. SSA SS1-89, US DHEW, July 1970.

Hamilton A, Hardy HL: Industrial Toxicology, 3rd edition. Acton, MA, Publishing Sciences Group, 1974.

Hunter D: The Diseases of Occupations, 5th edition. London, England, Little, Brown, and Co, 1974.

Hutchinson M (ed): A guide to the work relatedness of disease. Pub 77-123, US DHEW National Institute of Occupational Safety and Health, 1976.

Rivers W: The physician's role in disability evaluation. Continuing Ed 8(10):67-75, 1976.

Schwarts L, Tulipan L, Birmingham DJ: Occupational Diseases of the Skin, 3rd edition. Philadelphia, PA, Lea and Febiger, 1975.

Silver R: Occupational medicine: A new challenge to medical groups. Group Practice (Nov-3-18, 1977.

Mental Health in Communities

L. Ralph Jones, M.D.
Richard R. Parlour, M.D.

In the largely agrarian society of early America, most of the mentally ill were confined to poorhouses, jails, or kept secluded at home. In the 1840s Dorothea Dix spearheaded the reform movement that resulted in a shift in the focus of treatment from communities to state hospitals. Her goal was to provide "moral treatment" for the poor, but this goal was not realized. These institutions quickly became glutted with patients. Hospital staffs saw their budgets and treatment goals overwhelmed. The passage of years defeated all the initial enthusiasm. In 1963, President Kennedy described state mental hospitals as "shamefully understaffed, overcrowded, unpleasant institutions from which death too often provides the only firm hope of relief." He advocated " a new approach to mental illness, [replacing] the cold mercy of custodial isolation by the open warmth of community concern and capability... Prevention, treatment and rehabilitation will substitute for a desultory interest in confining patients... Central to a new mental health program [will be] community care."*

In the past 15 years, community mental health approaches have become increasingly important. What began as a system of clinical programs located in community facilities outside of hospitals also became a focus on the population in addition to the individual. Community mental health is concerned with characteristics of our mental health environment and how these affect the functioning of individuals, groups and society as a whole. Community mental health is also an attitude or orientation, a readiness to consider the impact of actions or events on the mental health of the community. This allows an emphasis on prevention and the promotion of mental health. This interdisciplinary field is concerned with a range of etiological factors—psychological, social, genetic and metabolic—and its clinical practice fosters the utilization of epidemiological methods in program

---

From Kennedy JF: A message from the President of the United States relative to mental illness and mental retardation. U.S. Government Printing Office, pp 3-4, 1963.

planning and in understanding issues which relate to populations and communities.[1,2]

History of Community Mental Health

It may be surprising to note that community oriented approaches have always been important in the management of mental disorders in society. The ancient Greek temple cults were actually therapeutically designed communities. The early Christian monasteries improved the mental health of surrounding villages by taking in unwanted persons. In the middle ages, city-states provided "asylums" for the mentally ill, ostensibly for the protection of the patients, but primarily to eliminate the health hazard and nuisance of unwanted persons roaming the street. These dungeons for the mentally ill are famous for their pratice of placing patients in chains and offering tours to spectators to raise money for operation of the asylum.[3]

Phillippe Pinel is famous as the man who "took the chains off the insane."[4] The atmosphere of asylums was made more humane as patients tended to behave in a manner befitting their surroundings. By granting dignity to patients, Pinel increased the healthfulness of the community within the hospital and the neighborhood nearby.

Pinel's pioneering efforts were emulated in England by William Tuke and in the United States by Benjamin Rush, Isaac Ray and others. Psychiatric patients who could pay private fees received "moral treatment", defined as kind, individualized care in a small hospital setting, with organized group living, a healthy psychological environment and opportunity for recreational and occupational therapy.[5] The segment of mentally ill persons served was narrow, and something had to be done for destitute patients who were clogging the criminal justice system and roving the city streets seeking food and shelter. The state hospital era was founded as a great humanitarian effort to improve community health by treating the mentally ill in places of refuge. From the beginning, new mental hospitals which were opened in most states were not given adequate operating budgets. Within the next 50 years, most state hospitals became enormous untherapeutic barracks. Most patients admitted to these hospitals remained for many years or for life. The population warehoused in these institutions gradually increased over the years to a peak in 1955 of 558,992 patients.

Early in the 1900s, Clifford Beers' autobiographical book, *A Mind That Found Itself,*[6] aroused public concern about the treatment of the mentally ill. At the turn of the century, there was international interest in new psychological and psychoanalytic theories. In the 1920s, child guidance clinics were opened in many cities, but these developments had little effect on the majority of the mentally ill or the custodial care in state hospitals.[7]

A new way of treating battle casualties was developed in World War II. In

World War I, the so-called shell-shock patients were treated like other medical or surgical patients in hospitals far from the battlegrounds. The condition was called battle fatigue in World War II. The soldier remained at the battalion aide station and maintained contact with his unit. He was treated with intensive rest, recreation, nutrition and the expectation that he would return to his unit. Less than 20% of shell-shock cases returned to combat, while 80% of soldiers suffering from battle fatigue did so. It was clear that the attitudes, expectations, and the treatment context greatly influenced outcome.[8,9]

The watchwords of community mental health, *immediacy, proximity,* and *expectancy,* were forged out of military experience. Treatment should begin before the patient has exhausted his social and personal assets; treatment should be provided close to the patient's home so that he need not sever important community ties (familial, occupational, fraternal, religious) to obtain treatment; the patient is considered to have a "problem", rather than a mental illness, and he will feel better once the "problem" is solved.[10]

The World War II experience, confirmed also in the Korean War, set the stage for a new psychiatric era in which state hospitals would no longer be the main vehicle of public psychiatry. In the 1940s and 1950s, the first changes occurred as new therapies were implemented in state hospitals; new enthusiasm was expressed for both treatment programs and the employment of more professional personnel. Major thrusts developed for outpatient and child guidance clinics, and increasing numbers of general hospitals established outpatient psychiatric units. Large numbers of nurisng homes were established, which served to relieve the pressure on the state mental hospitals for beds for the aged. Many innovations in treatment of the mentally ill appeared, such as intensive activity programming, "total push" for chronically hospitalized patients, and intensive treatment of the acutely ill. Group psychotherapy, milieu therapy, the open hospital, and various other programs for counteracting the dehumanizing effects of long term institutionalization did much to affect change.[11] The introduction of antipsychotic, antidepressant, and antianxiety drugs was most important in changing the methods of mental health care delivery. Their utilization in inpatient and outpatient care accelerated the development of new treatment alternatives to psychiatric hospitalization.[12]

The post World War II era witnessed the beginning of federal support for mental health. The passage of the National Mental Health Act in 1946 provided federal support of training and research in mental health. (In England, the National Health Service fostered community approaches to mental health care.) The National Institute of Mental Health was established in 1949. One result of the increased training and service programs was a dramatic increase in the numbers of mental health professionals during the 1950s and 1960s.

Congress passed the Mental Health Study Act in 1955 which established a Joint Commission of Mental Illness and Health. Its 1961 report, Action for Mental Health, advocated improvement of mental health care delivery by reducing the size of mental hospitals, augmenting their resources, and extending mental health services into the community.[13]

The movement toward community based care was given momentum by the enactment of President Kennedy's Community Mental Health Centers Act in 1963.[14] The Act provided for the construction and staffing of 1,500 to 2,000 comprehensive community mental health centers by 1980. Besides inpatient/outpatient care, partial hospitalization (day care), and emergency care, community mental health centers were required to provide educational services to the public and consultation services to the staff of frontline agencies such as police departments, welfare agencies, schools, YMCAs, and other community service agencies and practicing physicians. Legislation in 1975 mandated new services, including mental health care for children and the elderly, follow-up services for those discharged from mental institutions, arrangements for halfway houses for discharged patients and substance abuse services.[15]

Basic Concepts in Community Mental Health
Primary Prevention

The goal of preventing mental illness vitalizes the entire philosophy of community mental health, but to realize this goal a workable definition of mental health and disease is required for program planning and evaluation. It is not enough to define mental health as resistance to or the absence of mental illnes. A useful definition employs the following criteria: the ability to hold a job, to have a family, to abide by the law, and to enjoy opportunities for pleasure. A dimension of effectiveness and happiness is implied which goes beyond mere efficiency of life adjustment. But the complexities and dilemmas which confront preventive mental health require more specificity and precision.[16]

Primary prevention in mental health involves decreasing the occurrence of mental illness. In its application, primary prevention consists of both the promotion of mental health and the protection against occurrence of specific mental diseases. Evaluation of measures undertaken to promote mental health is difficult because of the complexity of defining mental health or the health status of populations. The etiology and pathophysiology of most major psychiatric disorders remain unknown, curtailing specific prevention strategies.[17] Nevertheless, some preventive measures have established their worth. It does appear valuable to prepare individuals in advance to deal with a crisis.[10] Various personality and behavior problems may be amenable to primary prevention through education to improve child rearing practices.

Certain mental disorders such as schizophrenia may require genetic counseling of family members.[18]

Another preventive measure is based on the concept that disease may be the result of an imbalance among a variety of social, personal, economic, as well as biologic influences. This perspective has resulted in a new approach to healing called the "holistic" or "wellness" center.[19] There are about 100 of these centers nationwide, but many individual practitioners have begun to incorporate holistic methods in their practice. There is an emphasis on poor diet, lack of exercise, and stressful lifestyle as precursors of physical and emotional dysfunction. Treatment approaches are addressed to prevention strategies, to the "whole person in his total environment", and may include nutrition counseling, meditation, exercise, and lifestyle counseling as well as medical or surgical remedies. These are promising beginnings, but breakthroughs in mental health research are awaited, which may be followed by specific definitions and specific program goals.

Secondary Prevention

Secondary prevention consists of early diagnosis and prompt treatment to prevent sequelae and to limit disability. Application of secondary prevention procedures to mental health focuses on four major areas: epidemiologic studies of population groups, crisis intervention services, public education, and increasing availability of mental health services. Recent advances in mental health epidemiology have followed the report of the President's Commission on Mental Health,[20] which documented that the burden of mental illness in the United States is very large. It may constitute our primary public health issue.

Previously, it was estimated that 10% of the population needed some form of mental health care at any one time. New epidemiological data revealed that 15% of the population were affected. Efforts were made to compare data on the prevalence of mental disorders with the utilization of mental health services. The current cost of mental illness is $17 billion a year, about 11% of all health care expenditures nationally. Of the 15% of the population, or 32 million people, in need of mental health services in 1975, 15% were under the care of the specialty mental health sector, 3.4% were under care of the general hospital and nursing home sector, and about 7% received care in both the mental health and primary care sectors. A surprising 54.1% were treated exclusively in the primary care sector. Another 21% of these persons were either receiving services from other human service sectors or not receiving services at all. In 1955, 75% of mental health services were delivered to hospitalized patients, most under the care of psychiatrists. In 1975, only 25% of mental health services were delivered to hospitalized patients.[20] The shift in the location of patients to the outpatient sector is striking, and the importance of the role of the primary care physician in the delivery of mental health services is apparent. Also, greater attention must be focused on the social and economic cost to those with mental disorder who receive no mental health services.[21]

The Physician's Role in Mental Health Care

A variety of factors have contributed to the enhancement of the primary care physician's role in mental health. The processes of community mental health center development and deinstitutionalization have accelerated the shift in the major focus of care of mentally ill persons from state hospitals to facilities in the community. At the same time, there has been a severe delay in community mental health center development and support of after-care programs generally. Also, despite the increasing numbers of such patients in the primary care physician's practice, many practitioners not trained in psychiatry feel inadequately prepared to deal with mental health problems.[22]

Fandetti and Gelfand studied attitudes toward psychiatric symptons and services in the extended family. They concluded that the extended family was seen as a frontline resource for advice on emotional disorders, but the next preference for a "gate keeping" role against mental illness was the family doctor. To a lesser extent, clergy, police officers, school teachers and friends were preferred.[23] This study and others confirmed the importance of general physicians, local non-medical helpers and the family in community health.[24] There is consensus that mental health training of primary care physicians needs to be augmented. Also, planning for mental health care should emphasize integration of mental health and general health care delivery, with appropriate division of responsibility for services to patients with mental disorders.[21]

Crisis Oriented Approach

Another important development has followed recognition of the special needs of individuals in crisis. Many individuals experience psychological "breakdowns" when confronted with unexpected or insurmountable stress. The treatment of stress-related disroders in World War II soldiers exemplifies early *crisis intervention* techniques. Stress reduction, symptom relief, and prevention of further breakdown by helping the individual restore self-esteem were the goals.[8] Lindemann and Caplan developed a theory of transitional pathology association with crisis states.[10,25] Both developmental crises and accidental life happenings may produce severe and protracted upset in psychological equilibrium associated with confusion, bewilderment, anxiety, depression or hostility.

Treatment approaches were based on facilitation of crisis resolution in the direction of healthy personality development and against psychologically unhealthy coping responses. The increased motivation to seek help from significant others and the increased susceptibility to influence for behavior or personality change in crisis situations were recognized. Crisis intervention has become important in all community mental health approaches, in community mental health centers, in physicians' offices, in self-help organizations, and in a wide variety of alternative human services.

Natural Helping Networks

People living in communities need a sense of neighborhood and belonging. All neighborhoods can serve to isolate individuals from the resources of society or help to tie them to its mainstream. A healthy society provides opportunities for people to be connected to each other to form associations of their own choosing and it provides special help for those unable to avail themselves of such opportunities. The "gate keeping" role is vital. Local neighborhoods may work in conjunction with formal caregiving agencies to enhance the quality of life and to provide a range of health and social services. The important ingredient is the orientation of the community to promote mental health. But despite the emphasis on community involvement in mental health decision making and programming, the community has not been effectively linked with the service delivery system. This shortcoming has resulted in a variety of peer oriented helping associations of people who share the same problem or life situation for the purpose of mutual assistance.[26,27]

Alternative Mental Health Services

The philosophy which became associated with civil rights, anti-war, the youth and women's movements of the 1960s led to the establishment of a group of alternatives to traditional health and social service facilities. These activist workers believed that, given the opportunity, ordinary people help themselves and one another to deal with most problems of living. They mistrusted services which labled or stigmatized those who came for help and in their work they tended to blur the boundaries between themselves and their patients. Alternative services were begun primarily by disaffected young people who worked as indigenous helpers in response to the physical and emotional needs of other alienated youth.

What began in the mid 1960s as a scattering of hotlines, drop-in centers, free clinics, and runaway homes, has become a national movement. Today there are 2,000 hotlines, 400 free clinics, and 200 runaway houses. These are organized by individuals of all ages, social classes and ideologies. The mission of these services has also greatly expanded. In the early years, these indigenous workers were preoccupied with providing emergency medical and psychiatric care, a safe place during a bad drug trip, or short term housing. In the 1970s, new community needs were identified including drug-abuse and alcoholism counseling, rape crisis centers, shelters for battered women, programs for the elderly, and various crisis intervention programs. The design of services has expanded from immediate care for individuals to include families and other institutions in the community. Houses for runaways have become long term residences and foster care programs. Some services define themselves explicitly as part of an emerging mental health movement, while others are wary of this affiliation. Many of these efforts owe their existence entirely to their political roots. The women's movement, for example, had its beginning within the civil rights and anti-war movements, but it has become a political movement focusing on the Equal Rights Amendment, child care, reproductive self-determination, new perspectives on sexism in society, and a wide range of individualized mental health and health services for women. Similar political and health initiatives are being undertaken by groups such as the elderly, individuals suffering with chronic mental illness and others.[28]

Tertiary Prevention

The aim of tertiary prevention is to reduce long term disability from mental illness. It has been found that severe disability is associated with hospital treatment under dehumanizing conditions, a state which is at least partially reversible by improvement of treatment conditions.[29] Even with the best therapeutic regimen available, some of the mentally ill cannot be discharged from the hospital. Others will recover sufficiently to live independently except during occasional relapse. The objective of psychiatric rehabilitation is to enable patients to make best use of the resources they have and to gradually develop new coping skills. Behavioral sanctions and social pressure may be utilized to move an individual toward recovery. Treatment settings may reflect progress at rehabilitation as there is less and less supervision. This may be applicable in terms of housing, employment, and social activities. Great progress has been made in the past 50 years in tertiary prevention, but there is a great need for coordination and extension of rehabilitation services into the community.[17]

The Rural Dimension in Community Mental Health

Community mental health dimensions change when a neighborhood is part of a rural population. Berry and Davis define "rural" as a small town or towns plus the surrounding farming regions. Boundaries are often diffuse and may contain a number of politically separate and competitive towns.[30] Bachrach reports that the usual problems of deinstitutionalization and community mental health are increased in the rural setting because of poverty, isolation, transportation difficulties, sparse population and resistance to innovation.[31] Rural persons affected by mental disorders seek no help 50% of the time. [30] Fear of being identified as mentally ill acts as an effective barrier to help-seeking, making the issue of visibility in a rural area a major one. Rural communities are also relatively poorer in community supports such as hospital programs, social welfare funding, halfway facilities, recreational facilities, vocational reeducation, job referral and medical care services. This makes family support and involvement more important, without which patients have few acceptable alternative lifestyles or job opportunities.

Rural community mental health centers are hampered by professional isolation of workers, lack of transportation for clients, communication breakdown in remote areas, and problems with outreach education in sparsely populated areas. Mental health professionals often encounter fear, mistrust, hostility, and apathy on the part of rural people. These attitudes may place greater burdens on family physicians and complicate referral. A community may be friendly at first, but then become recalcitrant when confronted with programs that bring changes that threaten the status quo.[30,31]

The Need For Reassessment of Community Mental Health Doctrine

From the beginning, legislators hoped that community care was not only more effective, but also cheaper than hospital care. The legislation based on the Joint Commission's report failed to heed the crucial recommendation for increased funding for mental health. Further, interaction between the mental patient and the community environment was more complex than anticipated. The first patients discharged were the least disabled and the best prepared for reintegration. Initially, deinstitutionalization appeared to be successful, but acceleration of the movement returned the chronically disabled, functionally marginal, alienated patient for which few communities were prepared. Many of the patients ended up in unlicensed, poorly supervised boarding homes or in isolated hotel rooms without resources for rehabilitation.[32,33]

The Joint Commission had recommended a detailed community after-care program and rehabilitation for an independent existence. After-care was not included among the five essential and legally required services until 1975. But though after-care services became mandatory, Congress failed to authorize necessary funding. As a result, community care services were not available to assist discharged patients in re-entry. Patients by themselves frequently lacked physical or economic means, motivation, or understanding to seek help. A social or emotional crisis often followed, resulting in rehospitalization for 40 to 50% of patients within one year.[34]

Of 2,000 community mental health centers planned, only 20% became operational. It had been hoped that federal support would be quickly phased out as local community resources took over. Subsequent legislation lengthened the period of federal staffing support, and the level of federal support was varied up to 90% for centers serving poverty areas. But state and local governments have not assumed funding of community mental health centers as federal funds have been phased out. The state hospitals are in shambles. They serve the most chronic, intractable cases and the numbers and quality of staff are low.[35,36] Inflation has led state legislatures to intensify pressure on administrators of state hospitals to reduce their inpatient census. Since welfare regulations have made socially disabled persons eligible for aid to the disabled and supplementary security income, states have discharged hospitalized patients in large numbers, transferring the burden of their care to the welfare system and the community.[33]

The tragedy is that in most cases community alternatives to hospitalization are demonstrably effective if they are adequatly financed and properly administered.[37,38] Community care has not been given a proper chance and instead there is a growing disillusionment which threatens a return to hospitalization and custodial care or abandonment of the mentally ill to the ghettos. There is a need for both institutional and community services, programmatically linked to meet the needs of the community. Further, there is a need to develop comprehensive human services which integrate mental health, public health, public welfare, youth services and corrections.[2,33,39] Conflicting state and federal financial policies must be revised in favor of patients. After-care and rehabilitation should be given high priority with emphasis on the individuals involved, the kinds of care needed and continuity of care. Finally, there must be consensus about programs and planning for mental health, avoiding mere transfer of patients from one system of institutions and funding to another. On reflection, despite 100 years of progress in public health and mental health, the goal to provide "moral treatment" to the mentally ill seems no closer to realization.[40]

REFERENCES

1. Hume PB: Principles of Community Mental Health Practice. In Caplan G (ed): American Handbook of Psychiatry Vol II, New York, NY, Basic Books, 1974.
2. Macht LB: Community Psychiatry. In Nicholi A (ed): Harvard Guide to Modern Psychiatry, Cambridge, MA, Harvard University Press, 1978.
3. Zilboorg, G, Henry GW: A History of Medical Psychology. New York, NY, WW Norton, 1941.
4. Ehrenwald J: The History of Psychotherapy. New York, NY, Jason Aronson, 1976.
5. Bockoven S: Moral treatment in American psychiatry. J Nerv Ment Dis 124:673-679, 1956.
6. Beers CW: A Mind that Found Itself. New York, NY, Doubleday, 1908.
7. Deutsh A: The Shame of the States. New York, NY, Harcourt, 1948.
8. Glass AJ: Principles of Combat Psychiatry. Military Med 117:27, 1955.
9. Mora G: Recent psychiatric developments. In Silvano A (ed): American Handbook of Psychiatry, New York, NY, Basic Books, 1974.
10. Caplan G: Principles of Preventive Psychiatry. New York, NY, Basic Books, 1964.
11. Psychiatric Services in General Hospitals. US DHEW, NIMH, 1969.
12. Klein DF, Davis JM: Diagnosis and Drug Treatment of Psychiatric Disorders. Baltimore, MD, Williams & Wilkins, 1969.
13. Final report of the Joint Commission on Mental Illness and Health. Action for Mental Health. New York, NY. Basic Books, 1961.
14. Community Mental Health Centers Act of 1963. Public Law 88-164, Title II. US Congress.

15. Community Mental Health Centers Amendments 1975, Public Law 94-63, Title III. US Congress.
16. Brown BS: Definition of mental health and disease. In Freedman AM, Kaplan HL, Sadock BJ (ed): Comprehensive Textbook of Psychiatry, 2nd edition. Baltimore, MD, Williams & Wilkins, 1975.
17. Zusman J: Primary, secondary, and tertiary prevention. In Freedman AM, Kaplan HL, Sadock BJ (ed): Comprehensive Textbook of Psychiatry, 2nd edition. Baltimore, MD 1975.
18. Dunham HW: Culture and mental disorder. Arch Gen Psychiat 33:147, 1976.
19. Ardell DB: High Level Wellness, an Alternative to Doctors, Drugs, and Disease. Emmaus, PA, Rodale Press. 1977.
20. President's Commission on Mental Health. Final Report. US Government Printing Office, 1975.
21. Regier DA et al: The de facto US mental health services system. Arch Gen Psychiat 35:685, 1978.
22. Shepherd M: Psychiatric Illness in General Practice. London, Oxford University Press, 1966.
23. Fandetti DV, Gelfand DE: Attitudes towards symptoms and services in the ethnic-family and neighborhood. Am J Orthopsychiat 48:3, 1978.
24. Dohrenwend B, Dohrenwend B: Social Status and Psychological Distorder: a Casual Inquiry. New York, NY, Wiley Interscience, 1976.
25. Lindemann EC: Symptomatology and management of acute grief. Am J Psychiat 101:141, 1944.
26. Caplan G: Support Systems and Community Mental Health. New York, NY, Behavioral Publications, 1974.
27. Naparstek AJ, Haskell CD: Neighborhood approaches to mental health services. In Macht LB, Scherl DJ, Sharfstein S (ed): Neighborhood Psychiatry, Lexington, MA, DC Health Co, 1977.
28. Task Panel Reports, Vol II. Alternative Services—A Special Study. US Government Printing Office, pp 376-411, 1978.
29. Gruenberg EM: The social breakdown syndrome—some virgins. Am J of Psychiat 123:1481-1489, 1967.
30. Berry B, David A: Community mental health ideology: A problematic model for rural areas. Am J of Orthopsychiat 48:673-679, 1978.
31. Bachrach LL: Deinstitutionalization of mental health services in rural areas. Hosp Community Psychiat 28:669-672, 1977.
32. Zusman J and Lamb R: In defense of community mental health. Am J Psychiat 134:8, 1977.
33. The Chronic Mental Patient in the Community. New York, NY. Group for the Advancement of Psyciatry, 1978.
34. Anthony WA et al: Efficacy of psychiatric rehabilitation. Psychol Bull 78:447-456, 1972.
35. Koz G: Catch 22: the psychiatrist in the state hospital. Psych Ann 9:5, 1979.
36. Knesper DJ: Psychiatric manpower for state mental hospitals. Arch Gen Psychiat 35:19, 1978.
37. Langsley DC et al: Avoiding mental hospital admission, a follow-up study. Am J Psychiat 127:1391, 1971.
38. Yarvis RM et al: Do community mental health centers underserve psychotic individuals? Hosp Community Psychiat 29:6, 1978.
39. Borus JF et al: Coordination of mental health services at the neighborhood level. Am J Psychiat 132:1177, 1975.
40. Scherl DJ and Macht LB: Deinstitutionalization in the absence of consensus. Hosp Community Psychiat 30:599, 1979.

Ralph Jones and Richard Parlour

Index

A

A Mind That Found Itself, 124
Accessibility, in good health care, 89, 90
Accreditation
  hospitals, 59
  health manpower, 72
Action For Mental Health, 126
Adequate compensation, in good health care, 89
Admission certification, in PSRO, 92
Age, in epidemiology, 30, 32
Air pollution, 107
Allied health workers, 69-71, 73
Allopathic medicine, 67
Alternative mental health services, 129
Analysis of community, 8, 9
Anthony, WA, 131, 133
Appropriateness review, in HSA's, 94
Ardell, DB, 127, 133
Asbestos and workers, 30, 31, 115
Attributable risk, 37
Atwater, JB, 101, 111

B

Bachrach, LL, 131, 133
Bahn, AK, 29, 43
Baker, WH, 7, 17
Battle fatigue, 125
Bed disability days, 20
Beers, CW, 124, 132
Berry, B, 130, 131, 133
Bias, in sampling, 48
Biological analysis of community, 9
Biosatistics, definition, 45
Blindness, in epidemiologic study, 40, 41
Blue Cross-Blue Shield, 79
Boards of community health centers, 16
Bockoven, S, 124, 132
Borus, JF, 132, 133
Brown, BS, 126, 133
Bruhn, JC, 8, 9, 17

C

Caplan, G, 124, 126, 129, 132, 133
Carnegie Commission of the Future of Higher Education, 1
Case control studies in epidemiology, 35
Causal association, 36

Kennedy, JF, 123
Klein, DF, 125, 132
Knesper, DJ, 132, 133
Koz, G, 132, 133

L

Lamb, R, 131, 133
Langsley, DC, 132, 133
Levin, LS, 62, 64
Licensed practical nurses, 70
Licensure, in health manpower, 72
Life expectancy, in minorities, 21
Lindemann, EC, 128, 133
Lung cancer deaths, risk of, 38

M

Macht, LB, 124, 129, 132, 133
Malaria, 30, 31
Master Facility Census (MFC), 63
Master Facility Inventory (MFI), 58, 63
Matching, in epidemiologic studies, 35
Maternal and child health, 104
Mausner, JS, 29, 43
Maximum Allowable Concentration, 120
McGavran, EG, 98, 111
Mean, in statistics, 52, 53
Measures of central tendency, in statistics, 52, 53
Median, in statistics, 53
Medicaid
    benefits, 82
    outpatient, visits in, 23
Medical care, cost of, 75-78
Medical care dollar, allocation of, 75, 76
Medical care evaluation studies, in PSRO, 92
Medical Insurance
    community rating, 78
    co-payment, 81
    coverage, 80
    deductible, 81
    experience rating, 78
    group, 80
    indemnity plan, 79
    prepayment, 80
    service plan, 79
Medicare
    benefits, 81
    outpatient, visits in, 23
Medicine, practice of
    women in, 66
    minorities in, 66
Mental Health, definition, 126
Mental Health Study Act, 126
Milk sanitation, 107

140

Minorities, ethnic and racial in the U.S., 19
Mode, in statistics, 53
Mora, G, 125, 132
Morbidity, in minorities, 22
Morris, L, 40
Mortality, in minorities, 20
Mortality rates
  minorities, 20
    accident, 22
    homicide, 22
  specific, 29
Mueller, G, 75, 81, 82, 83

N

Naparstek, AJ, 129, 133
National Commission on Community Health Services, 1
National Health Planning and Resources Development Act, 93, 94
National Institute of Mental Health, 125
National Institute of Occupational Safety and Health, 114
National Mental Health Act, 125
Natural helping networks, in mental health, 129
Nicholi, A, 125, 132
Normal distribution, in statistics, 54
Notkin, H, 13, 17
Notkin, MS, 13, 17
Nurses
  number of, 68
  types of, 68, 70
Nursing care, definition, 63
Nursing care homes, 61, 63
Nurse practitioner, 70
Nutritional status, in minorities, 23
Nutritionists, 71

O

Occupancy rate, in hospitals, 63
Occupation, in epidemiology, 32
Occupational health, workers in, 115
Occupational Health and Safety Administration, 108
Occupational health history, 114, 118-120
Occupational Health and Safety Act, 114
Occupational therapy, 70
Opticians, 68
Optometrists, 68
Outpatient care, 63
Outpatient services, utilization of, 23, 24

P

Paap, WR, 13, 16, 17
Personal acceptability, in good health care, 89
Personal care, 63
Personal care home, 63

with nursing, 63
without nursing, 64
Person centered care, in good health care, 89
Person-years, in epidemiology, 37
Pharmacists, 69
Physiatrists, 71
Physical analysis of community, 9
Physical therapy, 70
Physicians
distribution of, 72
medical, 66
osteopathic, 66
role in mental health care, 128
Physician's extenders, 69, 70
Pinel, P, 124
Place, in epidemiology, 33
Pneumonia—influenza deaths, 34
Podiatrists, number of, 67
Political structure, in the development of community health services, 14
Poplin, DE, 8, 17
Population, in statistics, definition, 46
Potato blight, 10
Pre-employment physical in occupational health, 118
Prevalence
definition, 28
relationship to incidence and duration, 28
Prevalence study, in epidemiology, 35
Prevention
primary, 42
secondary, 43
tertiary, 42
Preventive care, in minorities, 23, 24
Preventive medicine, definition, 3
Primary care, 63
Primary prevention, 42
in mental health, 126
Probability, concept of, 46
Probability sampling, 47
Professional competence, in good health care, 89
Professional, definition of, 71
Professional Standards Review Organization (PSRO), 64, 90
purposes of, 90, 91
premises in, 91
types of review in, 92
Profile analysis, in PSRO, 92, 93
Prospective studies, in epidemiology, 37
Psychological analysis of community, 9
Psychologists, 69
Public health
definition, 97, 98
basis for, 99
environmental protection for, 106-110
financing of, 101
health education in, 105

Systems, interrelationships in community medicine, 10, 11

T

Tables, construction of, 48, 49, 52
Tapp, JW, 2
Team care, 65, 72
Terris, M, 97, 111
Tertiary care, 64
Threshold limit value, 120
Time, in epidemiology, 33
Tuke, W, 124
Tertiary prevention, 42
    in mental health, 130
Two by two table, 36

U

Utilization of services, 23

V

Vaccine trial, 39
Variability, in sampling, 46
Variance, in statistics, 53
Vector control, 108
Veterinary medicine, 69
Vital statistics, 46, 102, 105
Voluntary agencies, 110

W

Water treatment, 107
Winslow, C-EA, 97, 98
Work related illness, 116
Workmen's compensation, 114, 117

Y

Yarvis, RM, 132, 133

Z

Zilboorg, G, 124, 132
Zusman, J, 126, 131, 133